D1648131

Also by Henry Grayson, Ph.D.,

Mindful Loving: Ten Practices for Creating Deeper Connections

The New Physics of Love: The Power of Mind & Spirit in Relationships

USE YOUR BODY TO HEAL YOUR MIND

YOUR MIND

Revolutionary Methods to Release All Barriers
to Health, Healing and Happiness

Henry Grayson, Ph.D.

BALBOA.
PRESS
A DIVISION OF HAY HOUSE

Balboa Press books may be ordered through booksellers or by contacting:

Balboa Press
A Division of Hay House
1663 Liberty Drive
Bloomington, IN 47403
www.balboapress.com
1-(877) 407-4847

ISBN: 978-1-4525-4501-1 (sc)
ISBN: 978-1-4525-4503-5 (hc)
ISBN: 978-1-4525-4502-8 (e)

Library of Congress Control Number: 2011963699

Printed in the United States of America

Balboa Press rev. date: 03/27/2012

TABLE OF CONTENTS

LIST OF ILLUSTRATIONS

ACKNOWLEDGEMENTS

So many people have given inspiration in the creating of this book. When in graduate school at Boston University, I talked a professor, Judson Howard, Ph.D., into letting me do a directed study on the research in mind/body medicine, since there were no courses in the curriculum on this subject in those days. As a result, I used my thoughts to stop a pattern of getting severe colds and sore throats three to four times a year, and have not had them repeat again since. Then, having Victor Frankl, M.D. as a visiting professor, I was inspired more than in any other course in my doctoral studies. Hearing his conclusion about the power of our thoughts, especially his stories about how many people survived the concentration camps or remained healthy, largely due to their thoughts and attitudes, has shaped the whole direction of my professional career as well as my personal life. Next, when in my postdoctoral training, my training analyst, Helen Durkin, Ph.D., continually helped me to look at the language of each symptom I got, discover the meaning of it, and find other ways to deal with the issue rather than paying the price of being sick.

And then some years later, a profound epiphany occurred while spending some time with physicist David Bohm, Ph.D., author of *Wholeness and the Implicate Order,* as I came to see the interconnectedness of everything in the universe. I learned that we are not locked in to a deterministic world, and that we also live in the quantum world where we have unlimited possibilities. Shortly after, I was introduced to *A Course in Miracles,* one of the most profound psychospiritual works I have come across, which states, "Your purpose is not to heal the body, but to heal the mind that thought the body could be sick," getting us to what is basic in healing the mind/body/spirit.

I am deeply grateful to the hundreds of professionals who have attended my training seminars across the country and abroad, helping me with their questions to shape my ways of presenting these concepts. I am most grateful to the hundreds of patients with whom I have worked, who in our work together taught me so much about how the concepts and tools presented in this book work in real life. And I am grateful to my dear friend and colleague, Linda Busk, who originally inspired me to reconsider our cultural use of the word "recovery," since we do not need to "re-cover" again the source of the problem. This concept fit so well into the basic theme of this book.

I have deep gratitude to the people who have helped with the practical parts of getting this book to press. Billie Fitzpatrick did a magnificent job organizing the material into this format and performing editorial services which made the book flow so much better. Sandra Oles, my friend, miracle worker, amazingly multi-talented assistant, my "right arm" in running all aspects of my office, has been incredible in researching and taking care of the hundreds of details associated with the printing, design, editing, and marketing of the book. I do not know how I could have accomplished this feat without her. I also appreciate the editorial work of Michelle LaPrise, Janet Ettele and Lisa Greenberg for the thorough line editing and catching unclear ways of expressing important concepts. And I am grateful to my family and friends who have been so supportive of this writing process, as I spent so much time writing when I could have been spending more time with them. I love all of you for your help, encouragement and support.

CHAPTER 1

Re-covery or Dis-covery?

Most of us say we want to be healthy and live happy, loving, and productive lives. Yet, in spite of this desire, most of us continue to suffer from innumerable ailments. The average person contracts a virus or cold several times a year, costing about $35 billion in lost work and irrelevant doctor visits for antibiotics which are of no help with viruses. We suffer from digestive problems, feel anxious or depressed, suffer from headaches, incapacitating back problems, depression, anxiety, or have chronic fatigue, just to name a few. Others of us suffer from more serious and life-threatening ailments, many of which can be prevented or healed, even some that are labeled incurable.

And further, doctors have been writing articles in their medical journals for decades about how to get patient compliance—that is how to get their patients to do what they need to do to stay healthy or heal. Doctors have told me that only a small percentage actually follow their advice for healing and health.

I have been working with patients in my offices in New York and Connecticut, traveling across the country giving seminars, and expanding my workshops to offer people a set of mindbody tools, techniques, and new ways of thinking that can literally restore your health, reverse many common ailments, and offer you a way to take back your power to keep physically, emotionally, and spiritually healthy. And would you like joyful, too?

Let me share a brief story about a discovery I made that brought these healing perspectives together into the shape of this book. I was about to begin a training seminar to a group of psychotherapists and healthcare professionals in Boston, when I made the intuitive decision to open the seminar by asking the audience the question: "How many of you would like to have a totally happy and healthy life?" Every hand went up instantly, agreeing that this is indeed what they want. I then said, "and with your permission, I would like to muscle test each of your arms to see if there are any barriers to having a happy and healthy life."

In my practice, I have been working with muscle testing for a number of years as a way to help my patients identify emotional and psychological blockages to healing, health, happiness and success in order to release them. Thinking of the philosopher Nietzsche's words, "the person we lie to most is our self," I had a hunch that even though the crowd of professionals before me thought they wanted to be healthy, that it was probably not true for a number of them. Indeed, *in spite of our consciously saying we want a certain outcome in our lives, including health, happiness, love and success, we are continually manifesting the opposite.* Muscle testing is a system that originated in the field of applied kinesiology (AK), is quite useful in getting past the lies we tell ourselves, to our inner truth or sense of deep true knowingness. We all have an inner knowingness or wisdom which knows what is true or false for us, and it shows up in our muscles becoming strong if we know a statement to be true, and becoming weak if we know a statement to be false.

Muscle testing was originally developed by Dr. George Goodheart and further developed by John Diamond, M.D. in the 1970's. Nutritionists use it to determine what vitamins or minerals you might need or foods which are harmful or good for you. And it is sometimes used by chiropractors who identify the disturbed organ by a particular muscle weakness. The practice has been verified by literally millions of muscle tests with people from most continents in diverse situations.

This is how I use it, which is a bit different from both nutritionists and chiropractors. I ask a client or participant to extend his or her strongest arm (one without any injury or shoulder problem) and ask him or her to resist me pushing it down as I press down on the arm at the wrist. I most often find the arm to be quite strong, especially if the individual is resisting as much as he can. Then I ask the person to make a statement that is obviously true, such as, "I am wearing a blue sweater" or "my name is Susan," and then press down on the arm again, finding the arm to be as strong or stronger in its resistance. Next, I ask the participant to make an obviously false statement, such as: "I am wearing a red sweater" or stating an inaccurate name. When the person knowingly *or unknowingly* does not state the truth, there is no resistance in the arm, no power, no strength in spite of their trying hard to keep the arm strong. When their inner knowingness knows a statement to be true, the arm becomes quite strong by comparison.

Every person in the workshop agreed to let me test their arms quickly on the two following positive and negative statements:

I deserve to have a fully happy and healthy life. vs.
I don't deserve to have a fully happy and healthy
life, and

It's safe to have a fully happy and healthy life vs.
It's not safe to have a fully happy and healthy life.

The results were quite startling for all of us. I had expected that perhaps 35-40% might have one or both of these barriers to a happy and healthy life. But astonishingly, without exception, *100% of the people in the audience had at least one of the two barriers and over 80% had both barriers to having a happy and healthy life!* That is, their arms were all strong on either or both negative statements: "I don't deserve . . . and/or "It's not safe to have a fully happy and healthy life" and their arms were weak on the positive statements, such as "I deserve . . . ." and/or "It's safe to have a healthy and happy life." What does the muscle testing reveal in this situation? That the great majority of self aware people in the room unknowingly had two very rigid, implacable barriers in the way of their having a fully happy and healthy life. In other words, despite their consciously declaring they "deserved a healthy and happy life" and it was "safe to have a healthy and happy life," their unconscious self strongly believed the opposite.

And these two barriers are only the tip of the iceberg. As you will soon see in the pages ahead, we all have multiple levels of hidden barriers that prevent us from getting well, staying well, and being happy. These barriers live in our thoughts, belief systems, traumas, emotions, and our bodies. The good news is that now we have the tools to identify and clear these largely unconscious barriers, which will reverse illnesses, energize our bodies and our minds to resist illness, and not feel at the mercy of physical symptoms or our out of control thoughts.

When I turned back to my group of participants, I asked them, "How many of you <u>are</u> fully healthy and happy almost all the time?" Only about 2-3% of the hands went up, which is the obvious confirmation of what the muscle testing had revealed.

This experience catapulted me on a quest to further explore if this was simply a curious isolated incident, or if I had inadvertently discovered an important clue as to why so many of us get sick or don't heal. I decided to repeat the impromptu survey when I was teaching a seminar in New York City. I wanted to make sure that my finding was not just limited to people from New England.

I was amazed to get the same result from New Yorkers: 100% had one or both barriers and 82% had both hidden barriers to having a happy and healthy life. This corroborated what I have found in my decades of clinical practice. When I also asked, "How many of you have healthy and happy lives most of the time?" only a handful of hands went up, giving further corroboration that they had barriers that were not conscious.

I decided to test this out again in other geographic regions away from the Northeast. A few weeks later when I was teaching seminars in North Carolina and in San Francisco, I got exactly the same results with Southerners and Californians, and then also those in Chicago and Austin, Texas. Finding that 100% of the people in all six samples in different geographic areas gave the same result, I concluded that we are dealing not just with a skewed population of people, but rather something that is part of the human condition, at least in the United States. The fact that we unconsciously do not deserve and that it is not safe to be totally healthy and happy is not so much psychopathology, but part of who we think we are. That day in my Boston seminar, I discovered just how pervasive and common these barriers to health and healing truly are. But even before, my clinical findings were in accordance with these polls, confirming that we all have multiple barriers to total health, healing, and happiness. So what's the problem?

We all know a huge amount about <u>what</u> to do to stay healthy given the hundreds of books, magazine articles, and thousands of doctors giving us helpful information about nutrition, exercise and stress reduction. The big question is: *why don't we do it?* How many of us have vowed that we will go to the gym and exercise regularly, but then do not? And how many of us actually think that it is necessary to go to the gym in order to exercise, which often "takes too much time"? For others it is, "I can't do it on my own. I have to be with others doing it." Why? How many of us have said we want to stop smoking, eating unhealthily, and drinking to excess, but do not? How many times have we vowed to get adequate sleep, but continue to be sleep deprived?

Even though both doctors and patients both know that regular exercise is an important part of cardiac rehabilitation, only about one third of patients continue to exercise in the long run. And even though it is clearly established that stress is a major contributor to most illnesses, and that meditation is a very effective tool for reducing stress, very few people take the time to learn it, and then only about 5% of those who learn to meditate continue to practice it on a regular basis. Many vow that they will talk in a more peaceful way to their spouse, children, or coworkers, but at the slightest provocation they lose it, reverting to their old unproductive patterns of communication. Many say they want a healthy, happy and fulfilling relationship, but keep picking partners who are emotionally empty or abusive, or they unconsciously provoke conflicts or create distance with their partners. Most people complain about the stress in their lives, but choose to do little to reduce the stress, internally or externally. There is something that is much more than a lack of willpower in this problem.

And yes, thousands of self-help books have been written about how to heal and be happy, and many of these books offer wonderful truths and exercises. These self-help books promise a return to a healthy body and mind, tell us what herbs or vitamins will make us healthy, what medical interventions (conventional and alternative) will bring healing, what lifestyle is healthy, and what practices to use. There is no shortage of information about the positive, self-empowering changes we can make. *Deeper questions remain: Why does this practical advice sometimes not achieve our intentions, no matter how hard we try? And, equally important, why do we not use the wealth of information available to us? Why do we not follow through on our commitments?*

Films such as: *What the Bleep Do We Know?* And *The Secret* suggest the kind of thoughts we should think, the beliefs and images that would be good to hold, behaviors we need to change all in an attempt to heal our inner selves and achieve happiness. Approaches such as the Law of Attraction offer encouragement, inspiration, and profound new ways to envision our power, but they are missing a most crucial piece of the puzzle: They do not identify or deal with the barriers which keep us from using their insightful advice to heal emotionally and physically.

I've realized that there is a gap between what these spiritually well-intentioned viewpoints promise, and the barriers we all have to achieving this promise.

We are now asking several questions:

- Why don't we follow all the advice?
- Why do the health-enhancing exercises often not work even when we carry out the rituals designed to create success, such as creative visualizations, affirmations, diet and exercise?
- And further, why do many of our physical symptoms or some of our emotional problems seem intractable, even after years of talking in therapy or taking medications?

The intention of USE YOUR BODY TO HEAL YOUR MIND is to address these life-saving questions. Over the past number of years, research has mounted in different areas of science; in physics, neuroscience, psychoneuroimmunology, biology, genetics, and mindbody medicine as well as in spirituality, and it has revealed the high correlation between developmental and adult traumas and the onset of illnesses, both physical and emotional. These discoveries have also pointed to the network of beliefs, thoughts, emotions, and even downloads of family patterns that underlie illness, stress responses, and the continuation of health-degrading behaviors. In short, if we do not identify and clear our barriers, many of which are not conscious, then thinking positive thoughts, holding positive images, and taking the right medications or supplements may be much like taking sailing instruction where you are taught about the angle of the sails in relation to the wind, the proper position of the tiller, and how it makes the boat move. But if no one ever explains that you need to hoist or cut loose the anchor(s) in order for the boat to move, you may not even be aware that one or more anchors are attached to the boat, keeping it from moving. In your ignorance, you keep trying and trying to get the boat to move, doing all the right things with the sails full of wind and the tiller pointed in the right direction, but still the boat does not move.

Forget Re-covery; Choose Dis-covery

We do not need to re-cover that which made us sick. Instead, we must dis-cover or remove the covering from as many of those issues as possible. As much as we declare our desire to be healthy, most of us have unconscious (though sometimes conscious, too), opposing forces or beliefs deep inside us, which fuel our need to hold on to our symptoms. Unfortunately, rational solutions and more information will not touch many of these hidden dimensions, which are embedded in memory cells from early childhood or even earlier. Cumulative traumatic or other painful developmental experiences as well as adult traumas are stored in the survival brain, the limbic system, as information and capture much of our energy, resulting in a reduced immune response. Numerous studies now show that there is a stunning connection between uncleared past traumas and current illnesses. This book will present a number of practical, effective and revolutionary methods for identifying and clearing out the effects of these painful imprints which will in turn free up energy necessary for healing and sustaining health.

When we get sick, we tend to blame something outside ourselves, such as "I caught that bug that is going around." Or we will project the power in our minds and give the power and intention to some part of our bodies, as in the statements we often hear: "my back is killing me," or "my stomach has been bothering me." Then, out of this false belief of a lack of power, we tend to run to the doctor to get the latest magic pill which we hope will cure us. Growing numbers of self healers have demonstrated that this is just not necessary and nor are so many of our more serious and even life-threatening illnesses inevitable. We do not have to live in the illusion of powerlessness. But then, as Ralph Waldo Emerson put it, "people only see what they are prepared to see." We hope that this book will aid in your preparation to see your greater potentiality.

From our childhood and adult pains and traumas, we might have drawn conclusions about ourselves, particularly about what we do or do not deserve and what is safe or dangerous. If, for example, we have concluded that "I do not deserve a healthy life," no amount of medicines can change that at the core level. The software, or underlying story or events that helped shape such a belief must be changed in order to give our cells different messages. If the belief is not changed, we will continue to have difficulty getting away from unhealthy life style habits or sustain healthy habits of exercise, nutrition, stress reduction, and constructive thought patterns. Consciously, most of us would say that we deserve a healthy life. However, as I discovered in my practice and in polls around the country that most people who have ongoing ailments carry not just one, but often numerous opposing beliefs as well as uncleared traumas at an unconscious level. I also discovered it by looking inside myself. Unless these beliefs and traumas are cleared, one's overall state of illness is unlikely to change in an ongoing way. This book will show easy and effective, but uncommon means by which we can identify whether we carry such unconscious traumas and beliefs, and offer simple and powerful tools which can be used for changing that internal software so we can have healthier and happier lives.

This is not a book about blaming the victim.

This statement cannot be made too often. Too many people have misinterpreted books on self-healing to mean that we must blame others or ourselves for being sick. This is the way of the egoic mind to divert us from our internal healing power so we will stay stuck in guilt or our suffering, or continue to keep getting sick. *But there is never a need for blame!* Instead, this is a book about finding, embracing, and learning to use our internal power to heal and to remain in health while *un-covering* more of our True Self in the process. Guilt would only make us more likely to get sick. And especially, it is the part of our minds which would keep us from embracing our immense internal power to heal and be happy.

Instead, we can take the unconscious use of our power which made us sick and use this same power instead for healing and health. This, therefore, is a book about how we can dis-cover, that is, *take the cover off, not re-cover the cause,* and use the phenomenal healing force within us which most of us have glimpsed only on rare occasions, and even then, only to a minor degree. You will also learn about a part of our minds which I call the false self or ego mind, that would like us to forever disown this power and see ourselves as victims whenever we get sick physically, emotionally, or in relationships. If we allow this illusory part of our minds to make us guilty or fall into blame, we can actually keep ourselves in the state of sickness.

In USE YOUR BODY TO HEAL YOUR MIND, you will learn specific techniques that you can do at home that will enable you to identify, access, and then clear underlying traumas, as well as negative beliefs, negative downloads, thoughts, and emotions. If you are a health or mental health professional, you will learn how to use this perspective and these techniques with your patients in highly effective ways. You will see how your unique cycle of interactions among these aspects of your false self are holding you and your patients back from true health, healing, and happiness. Even friends and family members can use them with each other. But if the problem is complex, it may be more helpful to find a well-trained professional to do the work with you. This is not meant to replace regular medical interventions, but to augment them. (In the Appendix you will find such resources.)

This book is not just about how we can quickly nip in the bud many of our symptoms, avoiding much unnecessary suffering, and heal ourselves from many symptoms that have already taken hold. But more importantly, we can dis-cover the inner causes behind our physical symptoms, and the barriers to letting them go. In learning effective ways to attend to them we bring about a more basic and lasting health and healing. Even more importantly, we can learn how to not feel victimized by our bodies and our symptoms, but instead learn from them, and access increasingly more of our own internal Power for health, wholeness, and happiness. We may not learn to prevent or heal from every single ailment, but what if we could prevent or heal 50% or 75% or more? And what if we could become happier, be healthy more of the time, and uncover our true Self, our inner healer, in the process?

How did most doctors and nurses in Europe during the middle Ages survive when they were exposed daily to the Black plague which killed one third of its population? Could it be that their compassion and desire to be of help made their immune systems stronger? Or could they have had thoughts that made a difference, such as, "I cannot get sick; I am a doctor." One historian explained the cause of death regarding the plague in Europe in this way: In Hamburg, 100,000 people died: 50,000 died from the plague and 50,000 died from fear. This insightful historian begins to take us to answers that are beyond the common mechanistic view of people and medicine, where the body is viewed as a machine and a body part is what needs to be fixed, and is largely separated from our mind and from Source. Beyond this old view, a new paradigm has emerged from the new sciences and ancient spiritual wisdom that sees an invisible, yet extremely powerful universe, one where *it is mind energy and consciousness that rules, not matter*!

Though not wanting to admit it consciously, many people, perhaps even most of us, want to remain essentially as powerless victims, seeing the cause and the cure of our symptoms as external. This book is for those who are tired of feeling powerless and tired of seeing any form of sickness as "happening to them." This book is for those who now wish to embrace their immense internal Power as part of the Source Energy and Intelligence of the Universe, who are ready to get past viewing the body as just a mechanistic machine with parts to be fixed, and find more ongoing health and happiness at the core of their being.

CHAPTER 2

Stop The Flat Earth, I Want To Get Off and Heal

*Somewhere, something incredible
is waiting to be known.*
Carl Sagan

How Our World View Impacts Our View of Health and Healing

"What is now proved was once impossible," wrote William Blake, whose words are just as relevant today as they were hundreds of years ago. It took a long time for our ancestors to believe that the earth was round and not flat, and that they would not fall off the face of the earth if they sailed too far from their known shores. People thought the Wright brothers were crazy, while others laughed at Henry Ford's idea of a horseless carriage. And who of our grandfathers believed that there could be communication by television, cell phones, and computers? They could never imagine that we could communicate so seamlessly without the necessity of some tangible observable connection.

Today we are in the midst of an even more shattering paradigm shift, one that is asking us to believe that there is an extremely vast, powerful, and intelligent quantum world we cannot see, but which exists nonetheless. This is not just my belief, but has been scientifically supported by physicists, neuroscientists, biologists, and other thinkers, as well as ancient spiritual teachings. This new world view has been espoused by scientists from the diverse fields of quantum physics, neuroscience, epigenetics, metaphysics, biology, and more; these thinkers have uncovered through research and medical and experimental evidence that we share an interactive relationship with one another. As physicists have discovered, there is no separation between the observer and that which is observed. We impact how each other feels and thinks. Just as we impact our environment, and our environment impacts us, there is also an active interplay between our genes and the environment. What does this come down to? We are all immutably connected. If we say something is impossible, could it be that we are actually saying, "I don't want to see it," or "I'm afraid of another world view."

Why is this important in learning to heal? Because how we view our world, our universe and who and what we are in it will determine much of when, where, how and even if we get sick, as well as much of when, how, and if we heal. Our world view will tell us we have limited possibilities, or that we have unlimited potential. It will tell us that miracles occur only occasionally, or that they are the natural order of the universe. It will tell us that we must predict the future based upon what has happened in the past, or it will tell us we are creating the future each moment with our consciousness. It will tell us that we are victims or that we are creators.

Everything is in a constant state of change. Such is the nature of the physical universe. But our consciousness can determine whether the change is to more of the same, or whether the change is a progression to something different. Does the change help to create an illness? Does the change revert back to the same to perpetuate an illness? Or does the change bring healing? In this new world view, it is consciousness which determines the results. Perhaps we can join Carl Sagan's enthusiastic openness about what is possible: "Somewhere, something incredible is waiting to be known."

Mainstream medicine and its theories of infectious disease are based on the germ theory as expressed by Louis Pasteur in the 1800's. He viewed the body as a sterile machine which would operate efficiently unless a foreign substance is introduced. Current theory based on Pasteur's ideas says that when specific microbes enter the body (germs, bacteria, viruses, cancer cells), they produce a specific disease. In an attempt to correct the imbalance, conventional allopathic medicine uses antibiotics, chemotherapy, and other medicines to attack and destroy these organisms, because, in this system of thought, if there were no microbes left there would be no disease. The commonly held belief is that our health can only be restored if germs that cause illness or disease are eradicated.

But the reality is that we are constantly exposed to germs, bacteria, viruses, and even have a certain number of cancer cells in our bodies. The outdated, mechanistic viewpoint does not explain why these cells multiply at one time and not another. Even though physicians refer to much of it as stress, as if it is an amorphous cloud hanging over us, rarely is it defined, delineated, or treated, except by a pill. Stress comes not so much from our circumstances, but rather how we perceive and interpret those circumstances—essentially how we react to them. Medical treatment of stress with medications does not take us to our internal power, but only temporarily corrects the surface problem in the short term, and contributes to our continuing to think that the healing power is external.

Another theory of disease also postulated that the environment was in part to blame for disease or illness. During the same period of time as Pasteur, this was the theory of the famous physiologist, Claude Bernard, who focused on the importance of the body's internal environment. In contrast to Pasteur's doctrine, he taught that microbes (that is, bacteria and viruses) could not produce disease unless the body's internal environment was unbalanced and susceptible to the development of the disease. The larger system of the body, the environment, must be sick in order for a germ to make us sick.

A renowned microbiologist, Rene Debous supported this basic idea, saying, most microbial organisms are already present in the body of a normal individual cause diseases. They only become the cause of disease when a disturbance arises which upsets the equilibrium of the body.

We must now recognize, as contemporary molecular biologist Bruce Lipton argues, that the environment of a cell is not just the material chemical connections, but is also consciousness, or an energy field of awareness, connecting us all to one another. In fact, as Einstein said, "The field is the sole governing agency of the particle." This means that the unified field is what influences what we call matter. And what is the field, but energy and encodings of information? This is what comprises the universe at an invisible level. It is what sustains matter. All of us are part of the field and cannot exist apart from it. It is not unlike what the apostle Paul in the Christian Bible acknowledged when he referred to God as "in whom we live and move and have our very being."

Unfortunately, much current medicine and the general population still follow the old viewpoint of Isaac Newton and of Louis Pasteur, thinking that they will get sick because someone sneezes on them or because a virus is going around. Interestingly enough, Pasteur himself condemned his own theory on his death bed, saying: "The microbe is nothing. The environment is everything." Unfortunately, the world did not hear Louis Pasteur's recant.

These discoveries do not mean that we should never take an antibiotic or have other medical interventions. Such medicines can often be life saving, or at least alleviate a lot of suffering. But we must recognize that they most often do not get to the cause of the dis-ease, treating the symptom or surface manifestation, leaving us to do other necessary exploration if we truly want to heal. And further, to think within the system based on Pasteur's earlier conclusions, erroneous by his own admission, helps to keep us in fear of the latest microbe germ or virus, thereby keeping us thinking as victims and that we are likely to be a victim again soon. Such a mental state, which is also part of the environment, could do even more to make us likely to become sick than the virus or germ itself, since the cell is influenced up to 100 times greater by the environment of energy and consciousness than by the physical environment, as Lipton points out.

What Controls the Genes?

For more than 350 years, we have lived by the science and world view of the brilliant scientist, Isaac Newton. His perspective was that the only thing that is real is what we can observe and experience with the five senses and can measure it. His new science of the time brought us many discoveries and understandings which have been very useful. It tells us how much distance we need to stop a car weighing 2,000 pounds and traveling at 70 miles an hour, and even how chemicals of one kind or another can affect our bodies. But again, what about all the exceptions? Newton is the one who outlined the laws of gravity, even though he first thought the idea that an object could affect another without direct physical contact was totally absurd.

In the early 1900's, Albert Einstein recognized some of the real limitations in this linear science, saying:

As far as the laws of mathematics refer to reality, they are not certain.
And as far as they are not certain, they do not refer to reality.

In this visible, linear material realm, if you knew enough about the past you could predict the future. That's the science behind giving a prognosis regarding your medical diagnosis, for there is no room in the Newtonian world for the role of consciousness in bodily changes, and certainly no room for creation or miracles which are possible in the powerful invisible quantum realm or spiritual realm. When something like this happens, doctors tend to refer to it as spontaneous remission. This is their way of saying it does not fit into the Newtonian scientific world view and therefore we cannot explain it. In the Newtonian system, the past repeats itself and we are locked into a deterministic world where we have little or no choice, but are largely cogs in a deterministic machine which grinds on and on and we support it with statistics from scientific studies. In this Newtonian world we experience limitations in every area. In this world view not only are we controlled by physical laws, but our bodies are also destined to replay the past, creating recurrences of symptoms over and over and in the way others in the tribe have done. We have little freedom to make a real difference in our bodies, and if it should happen, we call it a spontaneous remission or a miracle, not acknowledging that we have tapped into a much greater Source of healing power in the universe, one which we are a part of, not apart from.

For a long time we believed Mendel's understanding of the genome. We thought that so much of what we are and who we are is determined by our genes, and we believed that these genes are fixed, pretty much etched in stone. We were doomed to live out our lives as victims of our genes. But now the new field of Epigenetics say that our genes are quite changeable. We can deactivate some and activate others through our encounters or experience with the environment. Some of this activation happens without conscious intention such as growing up in poverty or some other form of trauma or chronic stress. Sometimes it occurs on a more energetic level in the uterus. But sometimes, this environment is also our own thoughts and mental activity.

How do we explain the man who was diagnosed with multiple personality disorder? When he believed he was one personality he had blue eyes. In another personality, he had brown eyes. How can this be? These things are impossible; or are they? If even one case exists it breaks the Mendelian law.

Consider another anomaly. A man in India and a woman in Germany have been observed and studied by many reputable scientists because neither of them has eaten nor drunk any liquid for many years. How do we explain their ability to exist without nourishment?

Are these examples miracles? Or could it be that miracles are the natural order of the universe and that it's our limited vision and belief system which keeps us thinking that they can happen only occasionally and randomly? Or that they occur only if an external and separate flat-earth sky god chooses to intervene? We no longer live on a flat earth, yet in many ways we think and act as if we are on that flat earth, for even our language still speaks of sunrises and sunsets as if the sun moves. Now we know much more than that the earth is not the center of the universe, believing that the sun revolves around the earth. We know that there is not just a simple universe, but also multiple and infinite galaxies, ever-expanding universes, and perhaps even parallel universes existing at different vibrational levels. We have trouble being able to hypothesize that we could be living in more than one of them at the same time at a different vibrational level. Why is it so difficult to embrace a new paradigm? Why are we so stubborn?

If we cannot see and measure something, using the 350-year-old Newtonian science, it is hard for us to believe it to be real. And that is precisely the old worldview which we must transcend in order to free ourselves from powerlessness. This powerlessness, or the attitude that springs from it, is that which ties us to our barriers to healing. When we begin to break down these barriers, we begin to open ourselves to the energy field and to our infinite power to heal.

We used to think of the world as having much solid matter—perhaps most of us still do. Yet, that is an illusion. We used to think there was at least a little bit of matter in an atom. Remember those pictures of the atom that your science teacher used to draw on the chalk board in school? The picture looked like a sun with planets revolving around it: the neutron was in the center, the electron and proton moving around it. We were taught that these parts of the atom were matter. Now we know they are just little sparks of energy. The startling fact is that when scientists smash the atom, breaking it down to its smallest parts, they find there is virtually nothing there except energy! This one example points to the fact that our entire universe is primarily empty space, which means all of matter is to a certain degree *just tendencies to exist*, as physicists put it, comprised of energy with encodings of information. They refer to this invisible realm as the unified field, which everything is a part of, including all of us.

Most of us probably think of our bodies as being largely matter, separated from consciousness, which is why medicine still focuses on the sick parts, understanding health in terms of illness. Yet, the body is at least 99.999% empty space, made up of molecules popping in and out of existence affected by consciousness; we are simply "tendencies to exist." What does this mean about our bodies' symptoms? It means that our bodies are not concrete or immoveable, but instead are made up of molecules that are constantly popping in and out of existence. What would happen if we knew that we could give these molecules different instructions? What if we could connect to our own consciousness (our human awareness) and direct them to heal?

All living matter—that which is seen and unseen—is in a constant state of change. In quantum physics, a quanta is known to be 10-30 million times smaller than the smallest atom, if you can imagine that degree of smallness. How many of us have ever seen an atom? At the quanta level, energy and what we call matter are virtually indistinguishable. At this level, it is consciousness, physicists tell us, that determines the vibration level, determining whether it remains as energy or whether the energy vibrations slow down to become what we call matter. The implication of this is quite profound, for our thinking, our beliefs, and our emotions can and do have a profound impact on what happens in the body. We can no longer see ourselves as powerless in relation to the body's symptoms, nor the body separated from mind, nor powerless against the influences of the world about us.

Perhaps we are seeing only a small portion of the real world and that this perception limits our experiencing miracles more routinely. Perhaps the real world goes far beyond what we observe with the five senses, and either is or includes the one which is not visible to us, the Quantum world. In this world there is immense power, even though we cannot see it. We can see the effects of an atom, as in an atomic explosion. But how many of us have seen an atom? How many of us have seen love? Yet we feel and see the effects of love all the time. How many have seen God? Yet many people report they have experienced the effects of their relationship to God, countless numbers reporting miracles in their lives as a result throughout the centuries.

We now know that whether we perceive something or not, depends on whether we have developed receptors to receive that information. For example, we do not hear high pitched sounds that dogs easily hear. The native Indians at the tip of South American thought Magellan and his sailors were gods having fallen out of the sky. They could not even see the ship with massive sails which brought them until the Indians were brought very close to the boat.

Let us look at another amazing discovery. According to physicists, zero point field is the place where there is the lowest possible exchange of energy in the universe—the most empty space of all space. Yet some physicists have hypothesized that only one cubic meter of zero point field contains enough energy to heat up all the oceans of the world to boiling point. Other scientists have described it as there being enough energetic power in one of our bodies to power all of New York City! What a huge amount of power in the emptiest of all spaces where there is nothing, no thing, meaning *that space, which is so void of the realness of the material world is where the greatest power lies.*

What Does the Quantum Perspective Have to do With Healing?

One may wonder: What does this have to do with healing and health? Everything! If we see ourselves, our bodies, our minds all as separate entities which exist in the deterministic world of Newton and the younger Pasteur, we are limited and doomed to much unnecessary pain and suffering, emotionally, physically, and spiritually. We are stuck. We are victims of germs, bacteria, viruses, our genes, of other people, and even our own body chemicals. We are destined to catch the next bug which is going around. Yet, consider people like Jack Schwarz, a Dutchman who helped Jews escape Nazi Germany. When he finally and miraculously survived the concentration camp himself, including numerous illnesses which were fatal to 95% of the people in his camp, he came to America. He was studied by doctors at the Menninger Foundation and UCLA medical school who found that Jack could drink poison that would kill most people, but he would not be harmed. I witnessed him hold out his hands toward a woman who had a severe migraine headache, sitting a few feet past me in a seminar. I felt waves of energy sweeping past my face and neck even though he was 15 feet away. She reported that her debilitating migraine had vanished completely in about three minutes of this energy. How can this be?

A Chinese medical doctor and acupuncturist in Stamford, Connecticut told me his family story of growing up in China. His father was a physician and practiced Chi Gong, and would have a Chi Gong master come to their home every Sunday to teach them. His older brother, being something of a prankster, liked to challenge things with the master teacher. Once he tried to sneak up behind him and tackle him. The master constructed an energetic wall around him which his brother crashed into, dropping him to the ground like hitting a solid wall. Another time, he tried to race quickly at him from the front. The master simply held out his hands, stopped his brother in his tracks with his energy when he was about ten feet away and actually flung him back about another ten feet.

How can countless Chi Gong masters do this and more, such as dissolving a tumor as you watch the CAT scan, just with conscious intent and energy? How can a karate expert chop through a stack of lumber with his bare hand without hurting it at all?

Our focus of consciousness contains more power than we can imagine if we only held it with pure faith. It is our collective belief that we are so powerless that it keeps us in powerlessness and so much sickness and misery, emotional and physical.

If you feel that you are ready to take charge of your own health, you will need to make a major paradigm shift, a shift in the characteristic thinking of the tribal beliefs about who we are, our intrinsic role in the universe, and what we are capable of doing. We will need to embrace the inestimable power in our minds and our thoughts to bring about healing, sustain health and happiness, or create an illness, which can often be considered to be largely a screwed-up internal information system. In many ways, this shift in thinking is far greater than learning that the earth is not flat and that the sun does not revolve about the earth.

In the Copernican revolution, people had to adjust to the earth not being at the center of the universe. In our new quantum worldview, we must come to see who we are and our role in this universe very differently: *we are integrally involved in everything and are continual creators.*

If our molecules are popping in and out of existence, or more accurately showing a tendency to exist, then why do symptoms continue in our body? Why are they not eradicated as our cells reproduce themselves? The information is just programmed in for its repetition, unless we change this information.

In order to get the results, we have to totally believe that it is possible to use consciousness for health and healing. What is necessary is expressed aptly in the definition of faith in Bible: "Faith is the substance of things hoped for; the evidence of things not seen", and in the phrase, "according to your faith, so be it unto you." Such faith is difficult for us, however, as Danish philosopher Soren Kierkegaard noted metaphorically, saying that when most of us take the leap of faith, "we quickly grab onto a limb and hang on to it."

Niels Bohr, the Danish physicist who was one of the founding fathers of quantum physics, made the observation that subatomic particles come into existence only when they are observed. That is, it is the act of observing which brings them into existence. If we "need" sickness, we will bring it into existence. It is no wonder that we have the adage: what you focus on is what you get. *A Course in Miracles* expresses it succinctly when it says, "the purpose of healing is not to heal the body, but rather, to heal the mind that thought the body could be sick." If we can let into our awareness the importance of such a perspective, we take back our power to affect what happens in our bodies regarding sickness, health and happiness.

Such a perspective was established by the research done by physicist Robert Jahn and clinical psychologist Brenda Dunne at the Princeton Engineering Anomalies Research Laboratory (PEAR). Accumulating enormous amounts of evidence from thousands of trials demonstrating how consciousness affects random generator, they concluded that the mind clearly interacts with physical reality, creating observable effects. And now, physicist William Tiller, Chairman Emeritus of the Department of Material Sciences at Stanford University has invented a machine, which can measure how consciousness affects physical space (matter).

A former patient of mine, while a student at the University of Connecticut, told me of an interesting experiment his psychology professor conducted with his classes. Four identical plants were placed in four rooms with equal sun exposure. All were placed in equal amounts and quality of soil and were watered equally. On each door to the four rooms were placed instructions as to what the students were to do when they entered:

Room 1: Talk kindly and lovingly to the plant.
Room 2: Shout obscenities of hatred to the plant.
Room 3: Play the Mozart music.
Room 4: Play the acid rock music or rap.

This student's mind was blown away by the results. He reported that in the rooms where the plants receiving kind loving words or melodic music were thriving spectacularly, while those exposed to hatred, obscenities, and acid rock were growing away from the music or people, and withered away rapidly and soon died, even though the material environment was identical for all of them. The mind was interacting with physical reality. (You can read of the results of numerous such experiments in *The Secret Life of Plants* and in *Secrets of the Soil,* both books by Peter Tompkins and Christopher Bird.)

And yet, we must remember that the science on which our current health-care system and even the thinking of a significant percentage of psychotherapists is still largely based on the old science of Isaac Newton, which sees little or no connection between our thoughts and what is happening in the body. This scientific thinking even breaks down the body into disparate parts handled only by specialists, though it is finally beginning to change. In the Newtonian world view of medicine, focusing only on what can be observed with the five senses, everything has a cause which supposedly predicts the future in a linear way. Such a perspective suggests that if we had enough knowledge about something, it could have been predicted way back up-stream. But this view is one of determinism, which does not allow room for free will interventions and the power of choice. We are little more than cogs in the great machine and are therefore just products of our past. Leaving little or no room for the role of consciousness and free choice, it leaves us mostly powerless in the massive and ever-expanding universes.

Relativity theory tells us we can observe the velocity or speed of an atom, but while measuring the speed, we cannot know the position of the atom. And the opposite is also true, the more we know about the position of an atom, the less we are capable of determining its velocity. This finding alone begins to break through the philosophy of determinism. But physicists in the early part of the 20th century still thought of light as waves. Then one physicist designed an experiment a little differently, and light turned out to be particles. This brought a tremendous amount of excitement in the scientific community. Light, which was waves, is now discovered to be particles! But then, when the original experiment was repeated, light was once again waves!

How could this be? Can light be waves and particles at the same time? To their consternation the physicists had to conclude that *whether light was waves or particles was determined by how they designed the experiment.* Could it be that next year someone will design an experiment which will reveal light in yet a different mode? Implications of these experiments for healing are enormous. How does a diagnosis affect a patient? How does it affect the ordering of energy through our minds to heal or stay sick? And especially, what is the effect of a prognosis? Does what we pronounce it to be, that is, how we design the experiment, make a difference in our mindbodies and in our lives? If you say, "I am getting tired," or "I think I am coming down with a cold," aren't you making each more likely to be the manifestation?

In the quantum world, and the spiritual world, thoughts are not so much statements of fact as acts of creation.

A story I heard from Professor Judson Howard in graduate school illustrates this point so vividly. Three baseball umpires at an umpires' convention were debating how they calls balls and strikes. The first umpire said, "Well, I just call them as they are." (The Newtonian view). The second umpire said, "It's different for me. I call them as I see them." (Einstein's perspective of relativity). The third umpire then voiced: "For me fellows, it is quite different from both of you. *They ain't nothin' till I call them*!" (The Quantum world view, which is also a spiritual world view).

Illustrative of the third umpire's perspective, I remember one man, a New York lawyer, who was diagnosed with leukemia. His family was quite upset with him because he continued to go to work as usual, not cutting back on his hours at all. He refused to face his illness, which made them more disturbed for him, thinking if he did not face it and cut back he would die sooner. But what happened was exactly the opposite. In his denial of the diagnosis and the prognosis of two to three years to live, he ended up working and living normally another 15 years! He designed the experiment differently from the doctor and created a different reality.

> *When a doctor is asked for a prognosis, perhaps he should answer with a question:*
> "What is your belief system about what you can do and what is possible?"

It would be far more accurate to tie in a prognosis with the patient's belief system, which he might choose to change, rather than making a pronouncement simply based on statistics, which may in itself kill the patient with the power of suggestion (the nocebo effect).

Perhaps the doctor should also ask before making such a pronouncement:

- *"Do you plan to clear out the effects of your past painful experiences and traumas in your life, since those are highly correlated with adult sicknesses?"*
- *"Are you willing to clear out the negative and limiting beliefs which can prohibit you from healing?"*
- *"What are you going to do about all of your negative thoughts?"*

The current way of making a prognosis does not allow at all for the power of consciousness and choice, but makes man a machine determined by the past, essentially a victim.

How do you design the experiments of your life? If you believe that you can catch a cold that is going around, you probably will probably reach out and catch it. If you believe that normal substances will affect you abnormally or that "there is danger out there", and particularly that you have to be at the effect of outside forces, you will probably suffer from allergies. If you attack yourself endlessly in your mind, you are likely to create an auto-immune dis-ease. If you pressure yourself endlessly, guess where it becomes pressure in your body, the blood and intestines. If your heart aches for love, consciously or unconsciously, but you do not become mostly loving, you can easily guess which organ is most likely to be affected. If you are often feeling powerless, your cancer cells are more likely to multiply. And most often so many of our attitudes, thoughts and beliefs are unconscious, since research shows that at least 95% of all our behaviors are unconscious. I will show you later how we can access more of them.

We have power beyond anything we have imagined, even though we most often live as though we do not, holding tightly to a belief that we are victims. When he was at Princeton, the eminent physicist John Wheeler questioned:

"Could it be that we bring the whole universe into existence through our Consciousness? The key act is participation."

Can we even begin to imagine that we hold such power? Physicists telling us that when we observe something we have already influenced it, makes us rethink the whole premise of what we call objective research. How much of medical intervention or the psychotherapeutic techniques is the method, and how much is the state of mind and energy of the practitioner and of the patient? Einstein adds to this questioning when he noted: "Not everything that counts can be counted, and not everything that can be counted, counts." This raises a lot of questions about "evidence based therapies." There is certainly much more potential beyond what we have observed and then called it a fact. We are constantly interacting with and affecting every part of our bodies as well as the world about us. In the unified field, we are all one, such as in the imminent physicist Erwin Shroedinger's statement that "the number of minds I have observed in the universe is one—a singulare tantum." Everything, including us, is just part of one Unified Field, totally interconnected at an invisible level. In the spiritual world, we all are also One. We are part of that which people have called God.

How much do our own views as well as doctors' and nurses' views affect the outcome of illnesses? Countless studies show the immense healing power in the placebo, a belief in an inert sugar pill or in the power of a suggestion or attitude. Usually we think of the power of the placebo as coming from deception. The patient thinks he is taking real medicine. But researcher Ted Kaptchuk at Harvard Medical School discovered a most unexpected phenomenon. His team asked patients who suffered from severe irritable-bowel syndrome to take a placebo. They were told that the dummy pill had no active ingredients, but explained that a placebo can improve IBS through mind-body healing processes. The participants were told that they did not have to believe in the power of the placebo and only to take two pills a day. The results: 59% of the placebo pill takers had significant relief while only 35% of the control group did.

The power is in the belief, often more than in the substance. We have projected our power onto the substance. But what about the nocebo effect, the power of the negative beliefs or thoughts? Edgar Cayce, the well known mystic healer of the last century to whom so many physicians referred their patients for diagnoses when they could not arrive at one, said, "Remember that thoughts are things, and as their currents run, they can become crimes or miracles." And eminent physicist Sir James Jeans states it so clearly as the central issue for us:

Mind no longer appears to be an accidental intruder into the realm of matter . . .

We ought rather to hail it as the creator and governor of the realm of matter.

And this realm of matter does not and cannot exclude our bodies. Being conscious of this new world view, let us begin to be conscious of our immense power, so that we can turn misery into joy, sickness into health, conflict into peace, challenges into growth, fear into love, and make miracles the natural order of our lives.

In the next chapter, you will begin to unravel the barriers that this outdated world view creates, so that you can begin to crack open the possibility, the power, and the potential to heal.

CHAPTER 3

Do You Really Want
Abundant Health?

The person we lie to most is ourselves.
Frederick Nietzsche

Accessing Our Power to Heal

A number of years ago when my youngest child was about three years of age, I was sitting on the floor with him opening presents on Christmas morning and I began to feel the pain of a pulled muscle in my back, and if that was not enough, I also felt a beginning sore throat. Having learned many years before that neither of these came by moving the wrong way or because of the bug that is going around, I told my wife that I wanted to take a little break and go into another room and do a little mindfulness meditation in order to see if I could dis-cover what was behind these symptoms. I did not wish to get sick, especially on Christmas! While breathing deeply and slowly, I asked myself, "Why might I need these symptoms right now? What would they get for me? What would they get me out of doing? What emotion are they expressing for me?"

The only answer I could get was that I needed rest. I returned to the Christmas tree and my wife inquired, "What did you come up with?" I told her that the only thing I could come up with was that I needed rest. She questioned: "Are you going to take a day off tomorrow, then?" I had been unduly busy that fall, writing, traveling and speaking, chairing a major conference almost single handedly, on top of a full clinical practice. Yet, I replied, "I don't do that. I never cancel my patients' appointments." Her response was so poignant: "Would you rather get sick, then?"

I thanked her for reminding me that I had a conscious choice. The cold or the back problem did not have to happen to me. I could take back my power of choice. I had been operating from the unconscious perspective that the only way I could give myself permission to rest by cancelling a day of patients was to get sick. Therefore my body would oblige me with not one, but two different kinds of symptoms: a cold and a back ache. When I then made a conscious decision that I would prefer to take a day of rest without using sickness as the excuse, and also made a firm commitment to do just that, which I knew I would keep, both symptoms went away within a half hour and did not return, giving me a joyful day instead of several sick days. If I had not listened to my body language, I could have been sick for days in order to have rest, none of which I could have enjoyed while paying the price of sickness. Even taking antibiotics, more vitamin C, or a muscle relaxant could not have worked so quickly and effectively, nor would they have gotten to the cause.

If you have a relentless inner slave voice that will not let you rest, which probably lies in some belief system you developed early in life, it may be difficult to make a commitment to rest. You are probably carrying a belief which will need to be cleared, such as, "I am loved only if I am achieving," or "I must always be struggling," or "I must be working to be worthy." Shortly after, I identified such beliefs which I had carried, and cleared them out so they would not continue to affect me adversely in the future. I will show you how to do this in a later chapter.

Being the Exception In the Linear World

How is it that when a virus is going around, some people get sick, but the overwhelming majority do not? Why is it when several people are sneezed upon, one catches a cold while most do not? Why does the sick one then say, "*everybody* is sick with that bug that's going around," when it is only an extremely small percentage of the population? How is it that doctors can make their rounds in hospitals, surrounded by all sorts of contagious illnesses and diverse bacteria, but rarely contract those illnesses? How can a person lift an automobile off someone single handedly in order to save the person's life, when we "know it is not possible" to lift so much alone? Some doctors say that we all have a certain number of cancer cells in our bodies all the time. Why do some people let them multiply enough to be what we call "having a cancer?"

On the other hand, why does someone who runs five miles a day for years for his cardiovascular health suddenly drop dead from a heart attack while running? Or why do some people have spontaneous remissions from a "so-called" fatal illness while others die? Why do some people living near a toxic chemical environment get sick and others living in the same neighborhood do not? It cannot all be genes, since they are activated or deactivated by the environment, both physical and energetic consciousness.

When I used to live in New York City, I would do running for my exercise in Central Park. I will never forget the faces on two different runners I saw frequently. One was a man pushing himself so hard his face was quite contorted, but he was moving fast. Another was a young woman who seemed to be floating like a butterfly just above the ground, with a happy and angelic look on her face, but moving equally as fast. In spite of this man's regular exercise, the man was on the verge of giving himself a heart attack. The woman was making all her cells happy with each step. Likewise, if we were to compulsively and fearfully require only healthy food, it could negate the health enhancing aspects. Mind rules above the exercise itself.

We must also come back to the original questions: why do we NOT DO many of the practices we know would help us stay healthy? Why do we not take supplements when we say we will, and which we know would be helpful to us, especially since our soils are so sorely depleted of essential nutrients? Why do we continue to consume so many processed foods which have the remaining nutrients stripped out. What is this something that seems to stop us from following other healthy regimens, even though we say we will do them?

Remember that one of the main reasons we have difficulty healing or continue to get sick over and over again, emotionally, physically, and in relationships, or even struggle with financial scarcity (which creates more stress and then illness) is that we have not identified and cleared the barriers, largely unconscious, that are stopping us from thinking, believing, and doing what it would take to be happy, healthy, and prosperous. And unfortunately, most of our healthcare professionals and many of our mental health professionals do not attend to these barriers at all, for it has not been their training.

The *New England Journal of Medicine* has reported that as many as 80% the symptoms that patients bring to their primary-care physicians are not organically based, but largely stress related. But the cause of the stress is rarely identified nor attended to, which means that the cause of 80% of our symptoms is not addressed! And further, it has also been reported that as many as 25% or more of doctor visits (all specialties) result from symptoms created by previous medical interventions, called iatrogenic illnesses. These include wrong drugs or effects of drugs, interactions of drugs, hospital infections, doctor or hospital mistakes, invasive tests, and others. In fact, medical interventions (iatrogenic illnesses) are a leading cause of death in our country, some say even ahead of heart disease and cancer. It seems as if we have deviated from the ancient medical admonition, "First do no harm." All of these illnesses place such an extra load on our medical system with many individuals and businesses having great difficulty in affording medical insurance, with costs of medical care skyrocketing. If we all take more charge of our health, we can take off much of the strain on our healthcare costs. *We continue to suffer needlessly from much illness that is not necessary, both by largely dealing only in costly ways with symptoms and by rarely getting to causes which are mostly unconscious. This book will show you ways to identify and clear them.*

Studies in genetics have shown that only about 5% of our illnesses are genetically caused. Therefore, from a biological point of view, says Deepak Chopra, M.D., "there's no reason why the body should be flawed . . . Having erased every outworn assumption from your mind, you are now free to entertain some breakthrough ideas that totally change the situation."

Let us use medicines and medical interventions when we must, for they have relieved many of our symptoms and have saved many lives. But let us use them consciously and cautiously, but certainly in emergencies, or use many of the natural alternatives to allopathic medicine which do not cause other illnesses ('called side effects.") Then, *let us not forget to search for the underlying causes and especially the barriers to getting well and staying well.* If we all did this, our medical system would rebound amazingly and we would all be healthier. We too often assume that telling a person what to do to get well will solve the problem, but, as noted above, most health-care professionals are aware of the widespread resistances people have to doing what it would take to get well even at just the symptom level.

How to get to the barriers to healing as well as to the basic original cause of an illness, physical or emotional, will not likely be given to you along with your diagnosis, whether from conventional or even alternative medicine. Instead you will typically be told how to focus on repairing the symptom in a certain body part only. The underlying cause is not likely to be attended to, for it often lurks under the surface, requiring ongoing and relentless curiosity and the deep desire to know—but without any self blame. While research has defined some of the origins of various illnesses, it most often does not get beyond the linear connection to something physical which could just be the surface manifestation. And especially, there is rarely any attention given to identifying or clearing the barriers to health and healing that virtually all of us carry. Alas, most physicians and other healthcare professionals are just not trained in this manner, since it is rarely if ever included in traditional allopathic or naturopathic medical school curriculums. Also, very little is presented in the curriculum in training psychotherapists, even though massive research findings in mindbody medicine are available. And then, many people are not yet willing to carry out this kind of curiosity, saying, "I just want the doctor to fix it for me."

Your deeper healing will come more from embracing a quantum scientific world view, a spiritual world view inspired by ancient wisdom traditions, or an unveiling of an unconscious psychological perspective. As stated earlier, growing numbers of self-healers have found in their experience, as I have found in mine, that repeated colds, viruses, backaches and allergies are just not necessary! Nor are so many of our more serious and even life-threatening illnesses inevitable and incurable as commonly believed.

Any time we use interventions which perpetuate the belief that we are victims, we set ourselves up for the greater likelihood of further illnesses. As we have said, this does not mean that we should never take antibiotics, other medicines, or never have surgeries, for sometimes we may not be able to get to the underlying cause of the symptom nor get to it soon enough. While I can often get to the cause of an illness in a few minutes or a few days, once it took me three years to get to the underlying cause of me and my family being infected repeatedly by Lyme ticks. (After getting to the cause, none of us was infected again.) I first tried numerous alternative medical approaches and then we resorted to taking antibiotics rather than have it develop into chronic Lyme disease. In such instances when we can't succeed in getting to the underlying cause, it is better to use the medication as an interim solution while continuing to search for the cause, such as the ones we will describe in depth throughout this book. But unfortunately, most of us do not continue the search, nor do many of our doctors or psychotherapists encourage it or show us how, mistaking the interim solution from the medical treatment as a permanent one. Wouldn't you like to have mostly perfect health? Wouldn't you like to be joyful and at peace most of the time? Do you know that it is a choice? But in order to have these, we must identify and attend to the underlying and often less conscious causes and barriers to health, healing, and happiness.

Perhaps Sigmund Freud was right 100 years ago when he said that we need to make the unconscious conscious. And as researcher Candace Pert, who discovered the role of neuropeptides in how the mind/body connection occurs, states it aptly, "your body is your subconscious mind."

Jenny provides a complicated example. She had been sick with multiple sclerosis for several years, and from the time of the diagnosis she had visited numerous doctors around the world to see if she could be helped. All of them had said that it was a degenerative illness, which for her was progressing at a moderate rate, and her physician said that there was nothing they could do to cure it. In desperation, Jenny visited numerous alternative healing practitioners nutritionists, acupuncturists, energy healers, herbalists, hypnotherapists, one who taught creative visualizations, and a homeopathic physician. Yet, her symptoms continued to worsen. When we did an assessment with muscle testing, which takes us beyond the answers in the conscious rational mind, we discovered she did not believe she was either worthy or deserving of being well, and also that it was not safe for her to be well. We also discovered that her mother was sick a lot when she was a little girl, and she would have to take care of her mother. The only time her mother would be nurturing to her was when she was sick. Her body was now speaking her needs to finally be taken care of. She had learned that it was not OK for her to show any dependency needs directly, so her body, her unconscious mind, was speaking for her. To let her symptoms go would not be safe! But if she became disabled she would have to be taken care of and she would not have to show her dependency needs consciously, which were unacceptable to her. With MS, she would finally get her deepest childhood needs met. Once she was able to consider it OK to be interdependent and allow some caretaking from others in a healthy way, her MS symptoms began to diminish and over the next year they disappeared. Jenny's symptoms responded so quickly, since that was the main issue for her which had not been attended to. Most of us seem to have to deal with a number of issues for the symptoms to abate.

Another example, Miriam, had hidden from herself the powerful symbiosis she had with her daughter, Tami. After developing several styes in her eyes, and finding that no medications from her doctor were working, she asked herself the Six Questions listed below. When she got to the fifth one!, "what is the metaphor?" she realized for the first time that she did not want to see the problem of the symbiotic relationship and the bondage it was for her and her daughter. As she became willing to face this problem directly, she realized it was a replay of what had happened with her mother, the causes of which she dealt with honestly. Her styes now healed and there were no recurrences, for she had gotten to the cause through identifying the metaphor.

Unlike Jenny and Miriam, others may have a constellation of issues contributing to their illnesses. Let us remain curious to uncover the causes until we get to the answer.

So many of our bodily symptoms can be translated into understandable language by just being open to answers to these six questions. Then we often have a choice as to whether to keep the illness by becoming more conscious.

My Six Questions

Whenever I begin to get a symptom of any kind, whether the sniffles, a beginning sore throat, a pulled muscle, a problem with digestion, an injury or accident, or something more serious, I begin to ask myself these six questions listed below. I know that the reality is not as simple as "I caught the flu from someone who hugged me," that "I pulled my back while bending the wrong way," "I must have eaten some bad food since my stomach is upset," or "my heartbeat is irregular because there is a problem with my heart."

You might be aware that you have been under stress. But stress, as we saw earlier, is not an external cloud hovering over us, but how we have thought about, interpreted, and reacted to external circumstances, people or events. If we can let ourselves know there is likely to be a significant reason behind the pain or symptom that caused us to be susceptible at that moment, once identified and dealt with, we can often be free of the symptom, sometimes in a few minutes. If we are not ready, or if we are afraid of embracing our power, it can take longer.

It is most important to start with even the smallest symptom in the body as well as the bigger ones. Consider this analogy: If you are driving down an interstate highway and you start to doze or space out from full consciousness and veer over to the edge of the road, you hit the little markers which give you a clear warning sound that you are starting to run off the road. If you heed this warning, you remain safely on the road. However, if you do not heed the sound of the markers you will run off the road. If that does not get you to attend, you will run into a ditch. If that fails to get your attention, you will crash into a tree, go over a cliff or fall into a river.

I believe the same is true with our bodily symptoms. When we overlook the little signals we get and fail to attend to the language they are speaking to us, they are likely to continue to build and then we are much more likely to get sicker sooner or later. We must continually remind ourselves of this reality: "The body is your subconscious mind," as researcher Dr. Candace Pert expressed it. It is telling us through the symptom, however mild or serious, that there is information from the subconscious mind that is important and needs attending to. If we ignore them, they will likely develop into something more serious, sooner or later.

Let me share an experience when I was in graduate school that prompted My Six Questions. It was a blustery snowing Saturday afternoon in Massachusetts as I was out in my back yard making emergency repairs on my fence which housed my German Shepard dog, a grandson of Rin Tin Tin. I was starting to get a sore throat. I cursed to myself in my best of slang saying, "Damn! That is the last thing I need right now. I can't afford one of those colds right now. I have to take my comprehensive exams next week." Since my early teens, I would have at least three to four debilitating colds each year. They would typically start out with a severe sore throat, develop into a horrendous cold, and often include laryngitis as well. Here I was studying for comprehensive exams and I needed all my faculties to complete my preparation.

Then I remembered the directed study I had done on mindbody medicine which taught me that there was a mind/body connection in a few illnesses. I was a bit surprised that I had not blamed it on the blustery weather, as we are so often prone to do. We frequently put the cause "out there" by saying "It's been so cold or so hot," or "it's been raining," or "it's the change of seasons," or "I sat in a little draft." I then thought to myself, "if there is an emotional component in ulcers, skin disorders, and asthma, why not in colds and sore throats? Is there something special about some parts of the body and not others?" It did not make sense to me. But I knew I did not consciously want to get sick. So I began to ask myself a series of questions, sincerely seeking truthful answers:

"Why might I need this symptom right now?"
"What would a cold and sore throat get for me?"
"What might it get me out of doing?"
"What emotion might it be expressing for me?"

My first and most obvious thought was that I might want to get out of taking the comprehensive exams. Then I realized that I was largely prepared, and if I postponed the exams, I would essentially have to start all over in my preparation and it would therefore require many more weekend hours of studying than if I took them now. I knew I really wanted to get the exams behind me so I searched further for answers, asking the questions of myself again.

At that moment I was aware of my neighbor looking out of her kitchen window which overlooked my back yard, and I felt a deep pang of guilt. "What could this be?" I questioned. "Why would her appearance elicit guilt in me?" Somewhere inside of me I knew that feelings of guilt could be related to getting sick with various symptoms. Then I got my answer. I knew that I had promised to do something for her aged father, which I was planning to do next week after my exams were over. I knew I would keep my word, so that was not an issue. However, I projected other thoughts onto my neighbor. I imagined that she was thinking: "How could Henry be out there in this horrible weather, doing something for his dog when he has not done what he promised for my father?" I then realized that my irrational ego-mind might be concluding: "If I got sick, I could justify my not having done what I had promised to do—even though I knew I would do it after the exam. I would then have an excuse."

But my rational mind said, "I don't need an excuse. I'm not trying to get out of this promise. I know I keep my word about such things. I have just projected other thoughts onto my neighbor. I don't even know what she was thinking! Would I like to deal with this conflict within me by paying the price of being sick?"

"No way," I concluded. "How would I prefer to deal with this situation, then?"

I decided that when I finished my repairs on the fence, I would go inside and phone her, saying that I wanted her to know I had not forgotten my promise to her father. Within twenty minutes, even though I was still outside in the cold, wind and snow, it never came back. In the past, the sore throat has always led to a severe cold, without exception, and now it was gone. But even more important, I have had another one of those severe sore throats and colds since that time, and it has been several decades. For, whenever I start to get such symptoms, I ask myself the same questions that I listed above, and have added two more questions. But I also found that discovering the "why" answer was usually not enough. It simply satisfies intellectual curiosity. I needed something more in order for self healing to occur. I found I needed to make a commitment to myself to deal with the issue in a constructive and responsible way that did not include the price of getting sick. I also knew that it must be a commitment which I knew I would keep, not a false promise to myself. Every time I did this, the symptom would go away. This was my first experience of discovering that I am much more than my body, and that my body responds to the thoughts in my mind. My thoughts create emotions, and negative emotions such as guilt can play a major role in getting sick.

The following six questions help us to do just that. These are questions I use endlessly, any time I get the slightest symptom, and have used them for decades. *Be sure to ask them frequently and sincerely, with a total degree of openness and curiosity, open to the most irrational answers, determined to continue until you get your answer.* Know that this is an important step, though usually just a first step, in identifying barriers to healing and health.

My Six Questions:

1. **Why might I need this symptom? And why now?**
2. **What do I hope it will get for me?**
3. **What will it get me out of doing?**

4. What emotion or need is it expressing for me?

5. What is the metaphor being expressed through the symptom?

6. What is the family, tribal or cultural belief involved in this symptom?

Examples: What is back breaking, or who is the pain in the neck, or does my itching mean I want to be stroked, or does my upset stomach mean I could shit all over someone because I am so angry at him? Or perhaps I need some love and nurturance which I missed as a child. Do I need to get the same illness as my mother or father in order to show my allegiance? Does my heart ache?

The next and most important step is to determine a more constructive way of dealing with these conflicts rather than being sick and miserable, but this works only if you truly choose and mean it.

The meaning of the answers to these questions is obvious, but *getting the answer alone most often does not bring about healing*, as I discovered in my back yard in Massachusetts that blustery day. I may observe that my house is on fire, but that alone will not put out the fire. *I find that I must make a clear commitment to deal with the issue differently, a commitment that I know I will keep.* It needs to be a solution which will clearly substitute in a more healthy way to deal with my wanting to get out of something or to try to get something by having the symptom. For example, like Jenny, if you discover that you needed the symptom in order to get loving attention, since that was the only way you ever got that kind of attention in your family, you may need to come up with another way of dealing with that need for attention instead of getting sick and paying that miserable price each time. Or if getting sick will get you to slow down and stop taking on excessive responsibilities, then instead, you might prefer to clear out the belief that you do not deserve to slow down, and then install a positive belief in its place, one which you would rather live by. *I cannot emphasize enough that in order for it to be effective, your healthier alternative solution must be one which you are absolutely certain you will keep and make a clear commitment to do so!* As I will show you later, getting rid of trauma or an old belief is much like deleting old software from your computer and installing a new and more desirable program in its place.

While your rational answers might sometimes be the answer, the true answer often lies in the most irrational ones, which you will miss if you discount them because they are irrational. No matter how far-fetched your answers may be, just let them come to the surface of your consciousness and make a note of them.

These answers can be one way of getting to some of your barriers to healing. As a simple and common example of finding an alternate solution to being sick, you might get the answer that you want some sympathy or loving attention. Would you want to pay the price of sickness and misery in order to get the attention? If you don't wish to pay such a price, you will need to decide clearly on another alternative such as when and how you will take care of that need, and then make a firm commitment which you know you will keep about how and when you will do it. Or have you been carrying guilt about something, repressing your angry feelings, or carrying a lot of worry and fear? The answer to these must be attended to in order to be free of the symptoms, which is often largely just body language trying to tell you something which has not been conscious.

We can let the sickness rule us and be passive victims, *or we can choose another way to deal with the need or emotion being expressed in lieu of getting sick.* Most often, I find that getting the answer to one or more of My Six Questions is not sufficient. As noted above, we must also find an alternative way of dealing with the issue and make a firm commitment to carrying it out which we know we will keep. It cannot be empty words, for that will not work at all.

If you are not sure of the validity of your answers, you can get confirmation or disconfirmation of your answers to My Six Questions, determining whether they are honestly true or false, by using muscle testing, which you will learn about in the very next chapter. Our ego minds can often fool us in order to keep us in suffering, making us think that something is not a significant issue, when in fact it is. Many people have concluded, "that is no longer an issue for me. I talked about it in therapy for years." But when we do muscle testing, the amount of disturbance remaining is an 8, 9, or 10 on the 10-point scale. While the talking therapy can help with many problems, many other times it may rehearse and reinforce the problem, particularly if it is a catastrophic trauma, a continual developmental trauma, negative childhood downloads, genetic memories, or an entrenched core belief. On the other hand, muscle testing reveals our inner truth or knowingness, which quite often is not consistent with our conscious statements. But it will be consistent with whatever symptoms or life issues that are currently being manifested. It can also help identify whether the answer you got is the complete answer, or whether there are other issues, which need to be identified in order to let go of your symptom or illness.

Becoming Aware of Your True Health

Just as My Six Questions are used to help us get underneath the why of our illnesses or symptoms, the following Self Awareness Questionnaire is a tool that will enable you to become more conscious and objective about how you think about your body, its health, and how you mentally frame the ideas of illness in your mind. (This Questionnaire is available in a printable PDF format on my web site for your convenience.)

SELF AWARENESS QUESTIONNAIRE FOR ABUNDANT HEALTH AND HEALING

<u>Remember to be honest with yourself.</u> If not, you are likely to prolong or keep your symptoms unnecessarily, or be more prone to additional ill health in the future. *Be sure to allow irrational answers as well as rational ones. Do not be critical of yourself over any answer you have. There is <u>never</u> a need for self blame.* Just consider all answers as opportunities to find more abundant health. NOTE: if you start to experience self blame or feel guilt at any point while taking this questionnaire, that may be one of the most important things for you to release, since guilt is a major contributor to getting sick.

NAME _____

DATE: _____

Since we are dealing not with a separate mind and separate body, but rather a mindbody, as you answer, think of health or sickness as including both mind and body dimensions of who you are.

1. Are you as healthy as you would like to be now?
___ All the time ___ Most of the time ___ Occasionally ___ Seldom ___ Never

2. What would be excellent health for you?

_____

_____

_____

_____

3. What would you gain by being in excellent health?

_____

_____

_____

_____

4. What would you lose by being in excellent health?

_____

_____

_____

_____

5. What do you lose by being sick?

_____

_____

_____

_____

6. What do you gain by being sick?

_____

_____

_____

_____

7. What would having excellent health cost you?

_____

_____

_____

_____

8. What does being sick cost you?

_____

_____

_____

_____

9. What does your health threaten?

_____

_____

_____

_____

10. Do you believe that sickness is inevitable for you?
___ yes ___ no

11. What is the strength of your desire to be well?
Circle One: 1 2 3 4 5 6 7 8 9 10

12. What would it take to be well?

_____

_____

_____

_____

13. How much of that are you willing to do so that nothing will stop you?

_____

_____

_____

_____

14. What do you believe causes most of your illnesses?

_____

_____

_____

_____

15. What is the first thing you think when someone close to you gets sick?

_____

_____

_____

_____

16. Who is in charge of your life?

_____

_____

_____

_____

17. Who or what seems to be in charge of your body?

_____

_____

_____

_____

18. Do you control your body or does it seem like your body and its symptoms control you?

_____

_____

_____

_____

19. Who and what do you believe you are?

_____

_____

_____

_____

20. How does that fit with your being sick?

_____

_____

_____

_____

21. What is the first thing you think when you start to get sick?

_____

_____

_____

_____

22. What is the second thing you think?

_____

_____

_____

_____

23. When I get depressed:
___ (a) I look for an external reason
___ (b) I look for the thoughts I have been thinking
___ (c) I look for someone or something to blame
___ (d) I blame my body chemistry
___ (e) I want to run and take a pill
___ (f) Other

_____

_____

_____

24. When and in what ways did your primary caretakers take care of you as a child?

_____

_____

_____

_____

25. What are the ways you missed being taken care of?

_____

_____

_____

_____

26. Do you remember ever being dependent or vulnerable and showing it?

_____

_____

_____

_____

27. What happened when you expressed your dependency or vulnerability?

_____

_____

_____

_____

28. Do you feel like you always have to be strong to be in control?

_____

_____

_____

_____

29. What do you gain by being sick?

_____

_____

_____

_____

30. If I were well, I would:

_____

_____

_____

_____

31. I don't want to do this (above answer) because:

_____

_____

_____

_____

32. I think that most illnesses happen to us:
___ yes ___ no

33. I trust that I have the power to heal: ___ yes ___ no

34. I blame others when they get sick: ___ yes ___ no

35. I feel guilty when I get sick: ___ yes ___ no

36. What is the most common approach you take to get well?

_____

_____

_____

_____

37. What is your lifestyle for keeping healthy?

_____

_____

_____

_____

38. What percent of the time do you adhere to it?

_____

_____

_____

_____

39. What emotions are you aware of feeling before you get sick?

_____

_____

_____

_____

40. I get sick ___ number of times a year (including colds, allergies, upset stomachs, back pain, etc.)

41. Re-count carefully:

_____

_____

_____

_____

42. I usually get sick when:

_____

_____

_____

_____

43. I look forward to people being sympathetic to me when I get sick: ___ yes ___ no

44. What did others in your family get by being sick (as you were growing up)?

_____

_____

_____

45. What did they get out of doing by being sick?

46. What did you get by being sick?

47. What did you get out of doing by being sick?

48. What did other members of your family say about getting colds or the flu?

49. What do you think or say when you get the first signs of a cold or flu?

50. What do you think or say when someone around you says, "I think I am coming down with a cold (or the flu)?"

_____

_____

_____

_____

51. What do you do at the first sign of a cold, allergy, or flu?

_____

_____

_____

_____

52. If you were diagnosed with a serious illness, what would you (or what did you) think or say?

_____

_____

_____

_____

53. If you get sick, do you tend to blame yourself?
___ yes ___ no

54. If you get sick, do you tend to blame someone else? ___ yes ___ no

55. If you get the flu or cold do you blame it on that latest bug going around? ___ yes ___ no

56. Do you have or have you had a significant illness in the past? __ yes __ no. If yes, what?:

57. What did (or does) it keep you from doing that was important to you?

_____

_____

_____

_____

58. What did it get you out of doing?

_____

_____

_____

_____

59. What did it get for you?

_____

_____

_____

_____

60. Do you have allergic reactions? __ yes __ no

61. What do you see as a cause of your allergic reaction?

_____

_____

_____

_____

62. Do you refer to them possessively as "<u>my</u> allergies?"
___ yes ___ no

63. Do you suffer from back pain? ___ yes ___ no
Do you refer to it as "<u>my</u> back problem?" ___ yes ___ no

64. What do you think causes your back pain?

_____

_____

_____

_____

65. Can you think of any metaphorical meaning to any illness (small or large) that you have had (recent or past)?

_____

_____

_____

_____

66. I often worry about getting sick. ___ often
___ sometimes ___ never

67. What emotions or attitudes are difficult or easy for you to acknowledge or express?

Place an "E" by those that are easy.
Place a "D" by those that are difficult to feel or express.
Place an "F" by those that you feel or express with great frequency.

Place an "N" by those that you never allow yourself to feel or express:

___ fear
___ dependence
___ annoyance
___ deprivation
___ anger
___ hatred
___ sorrow
___ grief
___ forgiveness
___ affection
___ sadness
___ joyfulness
___ love
___ jealousy
___ happy
___ rage
___ acceptance
___ anxiety
___ resentment
___ hurt
___ rejection
___ judgment
___ shame
___ shoulds
___ delight
___ mad
___ grateful
___ appreciation
___ pain

___ lonely
___ guilt
___ empathy
___ calm
___ passion
___ lust
___ compassion
___ sexuality
___ generosity
___ peace
___ embarrassment

68. I feel guilty when I get sick: ___ often ___ sometimes ___ never

69. How often do you feel stressed? ___ all the time ___ frequently ___ never ___ occasionally
How strong is your stress?
LOW ___ (1) ___ (2) ___ (3) ___ (4) ___ (5) HIGH

70. What do you see as the source of your stress?

_____

_____

_____

_____

71. What are your thoughts about each stressor?

_____

_____

_____

_____

72. I enjoy my work: ___ immensely ___ moderately ___ very little ___ not at all.

73. I am happy: ___ always ___ most of the time ___ a lot of the time ___ occasionally ___ rarely ___ never

74. Do you often say, "My" back (neck, head, stomach, etc.) is killing me? ___ yes ___ no

75. I have suffered significant losses in my life: ___ yes ___ no. If yes, please list who, what and when:

_____

_____

_____

_____

76. I had other significant painful experiences in my life: ___ yes ___ no. If yes, please list them with age of concurrence:

_____

_____

_____

_____

77. I have had significant accidents/injuries: ___ yes ___ no. If yes, what and when?

_____

_____

_____

_____

78. I have had significant surgeries: ___ yes ___ no. If yes, what and when?

_____

_____

_____

_____

79. I was abused as a child: ___ yes ___ no. If so, when and by whom?

_____

_____

_____

_____

If yes, emotionally ___ yes ___ no. If so, when and by whom?

_____

_____

_____

_____

If yes, physically ___ ycs ___ no. If so, when and by whom?

_____

_____

_____

_____

If yes, sexually ___ yes ___ no. If so, when and by whom?

_____

_____

_____

_____

ANSWER EACH OF THE FOLLOWING QUESTION WITH A YES OR NO FIRST. To get a more accurate answer, use muscle testing OR see if your head wants to move in a nod for yes or if it feels like shaking a no.

THEN ON A SCALE OF "0" to "10", HOW STRONGLY DO YOU BELIEVE THE FOLLOWING:
For example: "0" means you don't believe it; "5" means you believe it moderately; "10" you totally believe it. Pick a number between 1 and 10: (To get a more accurate reading than self assessment, use muscle testing if you can or the above method). ANY NEGATIVES SHOULD BE CLEARED WITH THE EFT OR THE EFTA IN ORDER TO ALLOW HEALING. (The EFT and EFTA will be described in a later chapter).

80. I am worthy of having a healthy life ___.
81. I am not worthy of having a healthy life ___.

82. It's safe to have a healthy life ___.
83. It's not safe to have a healthy life ___.

84. It will benefit everyone for me to be healthy ___.
85. It will not benefit anyone for me to be healthy ___.

86. This sickness is inevitable because it runs in my family ___.
87. I can be healthy even if it runs in my family ___.

88. I'm afraid of losing a part of my old identity if I am healthy ___.

89. It's OK to lose this part of my old identity if I am healthy ___.

90. I am sick because I am being punished ___.
91. I am free of all guilt ___.

92. If it is going around I am sure to catch it ___.
93. I will stay strong and healthy, even it is going around ___.

94. I will do what it takes to be healthy ___.
95. I won't do what it takes to be healthy ___.

96. I choose to be healthy right now ___.
97. I want to wait a little while longer before I am healthy ___. How long? ___

98. I am afraid of embracing my full power ___.
99. I am quite comfortable in embracing my full power ___.

100. I am afraid of losing my identity as one who is powerless to heal myself ___.
101. It's OK to lose my old identity as one who is powerless to heal myself ___.

102. I am guilty and need to pay the price ___.
103. I am over my guilt ___.

104. I will lose something if I am well ___.
105. I will not lose anything important if I am well ___.

Be sure to keep the answers to the questions above. You might classify them into the following categories to make it easier to do clearings of the barriers to healing as you learn the tools to use in later chapters.

Categories of Answers:

- Beliefs about how you get sick

- Your needs to get sick (secondary gains)

- Traumas which have not been cleared

- Metaphors your symptoms might be expressing

- The language being expressed in your body

- Negative emotions which need to be released in order for your mindbody to heal

- Thought patterns which support your getting sick and remaining sick

- Cultural beliefs about sickness and healing—what is possible or not

- Family beliefs you are playing out

- Beliefs about yourself taken out on the body

Chapter 4

Our Barriers to Healing
and Health

*The psychological rule says that when an inner
situation is not made conscious, it happens
outside as fate.*
C. G. Jung

*The miracle does nothing.
All it does is undo and thus cancel out the
interference.*
A Course in Miracles

Our Two Inner Voices

Most every culture in the world has put forth the notion
that there are two opposing voices inside us: one voice is
the voice of truth or Spirit; the other is a negative voice,
the voice of temptation, which opposes our happiness,
our health, our peace, our success and especially our joy
and true inner power. This negative voice has been called
different names by various traditions: the Hindus call it
maya or illusion—thinking what is not real is real. The
ancient Jewish tradition recognized the voice as the yatzer
harah, the voice of temptation to lead us astray, while the
positive voice was called the yatzer tov, the voice of truth.

Early Christians referred to the negative voice as Satan and the positive one as the Holy Spirit. The devil did not become an externalized personified creature with a tail and pitchfork until about the third century. Until then, it was largely like the Jewish understanding the internal voice of temptation. Sigmund Freud referred to the negative voice as the death instinct, which he called Thanatos. He also recognized that there is a part of our minds that makes us resist making the positive changes we say we want to make. In fact, he said that the purpose of a successful psychoanalysis was to identify and get rid of all the barriers to making the progress we say we want to make. More recently many others have called it the ego or egoic voice inside us. All of them see this negative voice, by whatever name you choose, as the one which leads us astray. This voice not only wants our death and destruction, but our misery all the way there. No wonder this internal voice has been called the wolf in sheep's clothing, the sly serpent, or the great deceiver.

But in spite of the knowledge of these two voices being present, few of us actually do anything to deal with the negative one, the illusory mind. Most of us live by this destructive inner voice a large percentage of the time every day, since it is the voice which seems to dominate the incessant chatter in most of our minds speaking loudest and first in almost every situation.

The ego voice is:
    The voice of fear and anxiety
    The voice of worry
    The voice of guilt and shame
    The voice of judgment and condemnation

The voice of littleness, powerlessness and victimization

The voice of anger and blame

The voice of suspicion and mistrust

The voice which tempts us to seek for satisfaction, peace, love and health outside ourselves

The voice of greed and grasping

The voice of struggle rather than ease, trust, and flow

The voice of regret

The voice of arrogance and pride

The voice of pain and suffering

The voice of deprivation and rejection

And above all, it is the voice of the illusion of separateness

The tail seems to continually wag the dog. Would this not be a huge barrier to healing and happiness when every thought is constantly stressing the cells throughout our mindbodies, since a separation of the mind from the body is impossible?

The goal of this book is to help every reader to move out of the ego mind with feelings of victimization in any and all parts of their lives and embrace the highly powerful inner Nature of which they are a part. *As much as we would deny it consciously, most of us seem to be afraid of our true Power and are much more attached to a world view that sees things as happening to us.* We, in our ego minds, are threatened at the thought that we are immensely powerful especially over our moods and our bodies. It seems we would rather hold on to the illusion that we are largely powerless and at the effect of others, of circumstances and of germs both for the cause and the cure. The Russian philosopher Gurdjeif expressed it poignantly: "You can call on human beings to make noble sacrifices for almost any worthy cause. But just don't ask them to give up their suffering!"

The body's natural state is health and our natural inheritance is joy. But our ego mind, the false self, which is the major barrier to health and happiness, is the part of us that believes we are separate, and with its mental and emotional barriers blocks this natural state, often causing us to seek out solutions which can easily make matters worse. For example, when I was told some 25 years ago that I would not walk again without back surgery because I had such a severely degenerated disc in my back causing extreme nerve involvement, I had to make a decision. I could have chosen back surgery as the solution, but knowing the statistics at that time that 68% of people having such surgery were worse off afterward, I did not like the odds. I preferred to be continually physically active. So I chose to seek out other internal alternatives for self healing, and they worked with no downside risk. Not only did I realize that I must change my lifestyle (needing to stretch along with running and meditating to reduce stress), but I also asked myself the Six Questions and discovered several emotional and interpersonal issues I needed to deal with more directly. As a result of doing that, I was skiing in Colorado two months later, pain free, even though x-rays showed that I should not be able to function; And I have been pain free since, for any time I get the slightest pain in my back, I explore My Six Questions and carry out the preferred solution. And now the x-rays show that the disc is fully regenerated which my doctor said could not happen!

The common solution today is to choose to use a drug which creates several other illnesses (nicely called side effects), or to agree to many unnecessary, highly invasive tests which create other potential problems, or to live in fear of multiple illnesses which are touted in Multiple advertisements or the ever increasingly greater numbers of diagnoses in the Diagnostic and Statistical Manual of the American Psychiatric Association. The ego mind would have us all pick solutions that often cause more of a problem while promising to help us, whether in medicine or psychiatry—or any other area of our lives.

Using the body, especially the limbic system, the false self gives us messages about how to protect ourselves from the pains of lack of nurturance, approval, love, as well as greater pains like constant judgments, criticisms, rejections, or even abuse and trauma. Yet, true to form, *the solutions the ego mind uses to get us to protect ourselves most often create more of a problem than the one it promises to solve.* Obvious examples are: "I'm too tired to exercise." "I'll do it tomorrow," or "I'm feeling upset, so I will drink a couple of stiff Scotches or smoke several cigarettes or take a tranquilizer to feel better." We all know what happens if we continue to follow those solutions day after day.

When we engage in self healing of our bodily symptoms, a much greater healing is taking place in the process. By first identifying and then clearing our barriers and then beginning to regularly monitor our thoughts and question any false beliefs that lead to or keep us sick, we are healing the mind that so often needs to make the body sick. As we heal the mind by taking back our innate loving power, we begin to heal our faulty sense of separateness from the All That Is. We also begin to own our True Self identity, which is the ultimate purpose behind all healing—to leave behind the illusion of separateness which is the basis of all suffering of mind and body.

Our true healing of mind and body will come if we are able and willing to open our minds and change the way we see ourselves and the way we see the world around us. Are we willing to risk letting go of seeing the world and ourselves the way most people around see the world and us? Are we instead willing to see ourselves interconnected and part of the immensely powerful Source? Can we risk seeing that we are powerful beyond measure? Can we take the time to see another realm of possibilities where miracles are the natural order? Could there be a better way?

As Milne in his classic *Winnie the Pooh*, captures so graphically the human condition:

> "Here's Edward bear coming downstairs now, thump, thump, thump, on the back of his head behind Christopher Robin. It is, as far as can be known, the only way of coming downstairs, but sometimes he feels that there really is another way, if only he could stop thumping for a moment and think of it."

The purpose of this book is for us to "stop thumping for a moment and think of it" in order to be happy and healthy. It will require turning your old world view upside down, perhaps as profoundly as our ancestors faced in giving up the belief that the earth is flat or that the sun did not revolve around the earth, or that there is a powerful invisible force between objects which we now so easily accept as gravity. By being willing to see the world from this new vantage point of Quantum Physics, or the ancient wisdom, we can begin to see that we have limitless potentiality for healing, health, happiness and success. And we can begin to identify and cut loose the anchors, which are holding us back. Are we ready to get off the flat earth and see a different one? The only price we will pay will be increased health and happiness.

Consider an analogy. Your old cell phone was quite an advance at the time, allowing you to make calls in multitudes of places you could not call from before. But what if you concluded that only calls can be made from your smart phone, when you can now also send text messages, e-mails, take pictures, send pictures, get directions and maps, and a variety of other possibilities. Could it be that what we have thought was impossible for healing is now possible, and we just have not allowed in that awareness?

The true purpose of healing is to use the body to help us heal the mind that needed the body to be sick, and to become aware of our True Self identity which is part of The All That Is, having enormous power for health and healing.

Our Internal Barriers

Since our internal barriers to healing are manifold, I will just list briefly a number of basic ones that often get in the way of people fully embracing their innate power to heal or be happy. Later chapters will expand on each of these in depth. Though many of these barriers can overlap with one another, it is helpful to distinguish among the various types of barriers.

Traumas

A major barrier to healing comes from the cumulative traumas and other painful childhood and adult experiences that we automatically store in our survival brains, called the limbic system. These emotional, psychological, and physical events are also stored in other parts of the body and energy systems, and result in the emergence of different developmental pathways, reduced immune response, and continued pain. A weakened immune system obviously sets us up for dis-ease, which is clearly substantiated by the high correlation between earlier uncleared traumas (both in childhood and in adulthood) and current illnesses. Traumas may not be only from remembered painful experiences, but often unremembered infancy and other painful developmental early childhood experiences, as well as birth traumas, intrauterine traumas, genetic memories, past lives, and even parallel lives. Such an awareness can also help keep us from the tendency to blame ourselves, which is so common.

Many of our traumas listed above include events that we cannot remember with our conscious minds, but are nevertheless held in the most basic cells or energy fields of our bodies. As you will see in the upcoming chapters, you will be able to access and clear these barriers with efficient, healing energy tools even when they are not remembered!

Negative Core Beliefs

Negative core beliefs are those ideas or conclusions we drew from our early traumas that subsequently underlie and reinforce the pain of the trauma. Such beliefs as I don't deserve to be healthy and happy, "It's not safe to be healthy and happy," and "I'm not worthy of being healthy and happy," are just a few examples of beliefs that not only get in the way of health and healing but keep the egoic, victim mindset in place, disempowering us.

Other examples of negative core beliefs include: "The only way I can stop and rest is if I am sick," "Being sick will get me love and nurturance," "I have to get the same illnesses my family gets," "I am not good enough" and many others. Some of these can be quite strong, almost acting as a force against positive, health-emerging thoughts and beliefs. When we have deep seated negative beliefs, our internal energy polarities can become reversed, and instead of attracting health and happiness, we can actually repel it.

We can also hold beliefs from the tribe around us, such as "I catch a cold from someone around me who has one," "my body has to break down with aging," "cancer just happens as bad luck," "my back went out because I just bent the wrong way," "If I push myself to run 10 miles every day, I won't get a heart attack," and then you get one as you push yourself running. Our attitude helps more than the exercise, or it uses the experience to hurt us.

The bad news is that we will attract confirmation of these beliefs. The great news is that we also have the power to change these entrenched tribal beliefs. It is often almost as simple as changing software in your computer as I will show you later. Changing beliefs can help to make and keep you healthy.

When we are bombarded with suggestions from the tribe and the media, we unwittingly absorb a negative internal operating system that acts as a barrier against healing and health. For example, I saw a great increase in allergic responses when drug companies started to sponsor the allergy report on radio and TV stations along with the traffic and weather reports. Both the sale of cigarettes and deaths from lung cancer increased after the announcement of the research finding that smoking causes lung cancer. Such information does not seem to help keep us from getting sick, but often helps us create more sickness, affirming the old adage: *What you focus on is what you will get.* What does a cancer support group actually support? Look at the words carefully. Why not have a healing group instead?

Also, when we fight against something, we may unwittingly create more of what we think we are fighting because the energy invested against is actually attracting, not repelling. The body, your right brain, and the universe do not respond to the "not," but just to your focus and energy. The discoveries from ancient wisdom as well as quantum physics suggest that the fighting against approach of allopathic medicine just might often increase the problem, especially since physicists remind us that the minute we observe something we are affecting it.

By observing a condition with the attitude of fighting against or battling, as the media usually refers to one as "battling" or "fighting" cancer, we could be actually attracting more cancer by empowering what we battle against. Using such an awareness, Mother Teresa was once asked why she would not go to an anti-war demonstration. Her answer was, "when there is a demonstration for peace, I will attend." An anti-war demonstration can often carry the same negative energy as war itself. Consider, for example, the violent protestations of abortion clinics, attacks that supposedly value life.

Negative Emotions

Any negative emotion we do not deal with directly or let go of through meditation, therapy, or other energetic healing techniques stays stuck in our mindbodies, creating vigorous barriers to health and healing. If we suppress our anger, or if we frequently rehearse our anger, either extreme helps to create illness. If we do not consciously acknowledge and attend to our fearful and other vulnerable feelings, such as men are taught not to do in our culture, then we get sick or die from heart attacks earlier than women who are allowed to feel more of the softer or vulnerable emotions. Guilt often produces attacks upon our bodies as punishment, making us sicker. If we do not consciously acknowledge all our negative emotions with love and acceptance (the higher emotions), and then discover healthy ways of expressing them and letting them go, these emotions will not only be a barrier to health and healing, but as tons of research shows, produce diverse illnesses as well, for each negative emotion communicates immediately with all the 70 trillion cells in the body, making each of them unhappy.

When we live with resentment and do not practice forgiveness, we are holding on to the emotional injuries that triggered these responses. By staying attached to these negative feelings we keep the cells in our bodies in the state of negativity rather than at peace, setting up potential illnesses. Resentments keep us vigilant against other hurts, which then keeps our stress hormones unnecessarily active, diminishing our immune response.

Negative Thoughts and Identities

Harboring and rehearsing negative thoughts constantly affects every cell in our bodies through the neuropeptides, the body's instant messaging system. There is no such thing as an idle thought, for each one is communicating energetically up to 100 times more powerfully to each cell than the physical environment of the cell—even more than the physical environment supplied by a medication, as pointed out by biologist Bruce Lipton. I will show you later how you can become mindful of your damaging thoughts and give you effective tools to change them.

The power of our thoughts is evidenced in our unconscious attachment to our illness or diagnosis, which can act as a huge barrier to healing. Our sickness can easily become a part of our identity, part of who and what we think we are. How can we begin to let go of our cherished identity? Also, we often are quite possessive of our diagnoses, referring almost proudly and possessively to our identifications: my allergies, my asthma, my diabetes, or my bad heart, my weight problem, and so on. These identifications with illness are further reinforced when a doctor makes a pronouncement about a diagnosis suggesting ownership: You have irritable bowel syndrome, cancer, depression, allergies, pneumonia, a weak heart, or an ulcer, *[fill in the blank]. Such labels, along with the "my" or "have," reinforce the idea that we own or possess an illness like we would a house, a car, a face. We want to protect things we own. Some illnesses can sometimes be an identification with or allegiance to our families when others have had similar illnesses, which can further complicate our ability to let go of an illness, as if we would lose our family connection. Therefore such old identities and allegiances need to be cleared, for they are often a barrier to healing and health. And when we treat these allegiances as thoughts that can be cleared, we open ourselves to the possibility of being in charge of our health.

Secondary Gains

Doctors have long recognized the common presence of what they call secondary gains but rarely are they dealt with. This simply means that we feel there is some benefit, rational or irrational, conscious or unconscious, from being sick. It gets me something or gets me out of something. Jonathan, for example, had felt emotionally and sexually deprived because his new bride Cynthia had become seriously ill shortly after their wedding. His bride's mother had always said that her life ended when she got married. Could it be why Cynthia almost died from toxoplasmosis right after getting married?

Using Your Body As a Lens

Every sensation and symptom in the body is an opportunity to address or access the barriers hidden within. I will show you to use your body's symptoms as language to be translated and deciphered, so that you can use this powerful tool as a means to staying healthy, reversing an illness, and achieving well being in all ways. If we do not heed the markers on the edge of a super highway and get back in our lane, we are likely to run off the road, go into a ditch, crash into a tree, or fall off a mountain or into a river. Would we go to the highway department and try to get them to remove these little ruts at the edge of the highway so they won't trouble us? Hardly. The same is true with our body signals which we routinely ignore or cover up with drugs. When we ignore the little nudges that we are not feeling well or we rush to the doctor to ask him to get rid of our pesky symptoms, we are not taking time to translate and heed what these bodily messages are saying and then, where and when we might crash?

Our Most Basic Barrier

Our most basic barrier to all healing is an archaic and erroneous view of ourselves and the world that we are separate. As we saw earlier, it is a view based on the over 300-year-old science of Isaac Newton, which states that the only thing which is real is what can be observed and/or measured by the five senses. It is a view of the world where that which is not visible does not exist, and one in which our potential is limited rather than limitless and where our past determines our future. Unless we can embrace the incredible power of the Unified Field, (or our Divine Nature) knowing *we are part of it, not apart from* it, we will keep ourselves in the illusion of separateness, littleness and therefore in victimization, for feelings of powerlessness are central in many illnesses, physical and emotional. Disowning this internal Power is the basic barrier to health and healing. *This is why we need to use our bodies to heal our minds that believed we are separate, and therefore needed our bodies to be sick.* We must heal our illusion of separateness from Source power and energy, and remember that we are connected to The All That Is. The first step is to begin to recognize which internal voice we are listening to and following as our guide.

Identifying Your Barriers to Health and Healing

Again, since most of us are not always in a perfect state of happiness and health, and since so many of us do not do what we know is helpful to keep ourselves in total health and happiness, even if we say we will, we can easily assume that most of us have some of these diverse barriers. Jane had gotten strep throat several times a year for many years starting in adolescence. She grew up in a very strict home where her mother demanded compliant behavior about every little thing. There was no room for Jane to express any of her feelings, she just had to follow the rules. It was after she started to express a little rebellion that she got her first sore throat.

As an adult, Jane had difficulty in allowing herself success at work and in relationships, and her strep throats continued. She had learned that meditation strengthened the immune system, but she was unable to keep up the practice. She had learned that sleep deprivation weakened the immune system, but she continued to stay up late on the computer unless she was out partying with friends, ending up sleep deprived either way. She also had difficulty in her choice of men, picking men who were either distant or critical. Essentially, she was not able to consistently take good care of herself in many important ways.

We discovered that Jane had not only grown up with the trauma of having to be perfect and experiencing that there was no room for her emotions, but had then concluded as a little girl that she did not deserve to be healthy, happy and successful. Nor were health, happiness and success safe for her. She had concluded, as most little kids do, that if she was not doing things perfectly for her mother, then she must not deserve good things. She also had concluded that she should not express her feelings and needs in the world, for it would not be safe.

However, together, as we began to name the traumas and her reactions to these emotional experiences, we were able to begin to do clearing work. Once these traumas and the negative beliefs that grew out of them were cleared Jane found she was much more able to take care of herself through a regular meditation practice and sleep to not only keep her away from strep throats but feeling more healthy and energetic. She had learned to re-energize and strengthen her immune system. (In Chapter Four, you will see how these trauma-clearing exercises work and how you can identify any traumas from your past big or small so that you can remove these barriers to allow your true healing.)

Muscle Testing

As I've mentioned early in the book, I use muscle testing in a variety of ways, for a variety of purposes; however, one of its most powerful applications is to identify our barriers to total health, healing and happiness. Indeed, Muscle Testing (from Applied Kinesiology) is one of the most quick, efficient and effective ways to clarify your inner truth and get in touch with exactly what you believe or what is in your way.

In order for muscle testing to work, however, you may have to open your mind and allow the possibility that something which may seem weird can work and bring you tremendous comfort and healing. Remember, the ego mind will not want you to learn or use anything which could help you to be free of emotional or physical suffering and take you into health and happiness. But if you want peace, healing, and happiness above all else, you will be willing to do anything which has no harmful side effects and is not illegal or unethical. The false self mind will want you to use newness or weirdness as a means to not use something which will help take you out of pain and suffering.

Sometimes, to lose your old belief might be more painful and disturbing than the illness, therefore we might rather keep it. The important question for us is: Can I allow myself to have an open mind to consider a strange possibility which could help me, or would I rather stay in suffering in allegiance to my false self which would want me to not open up my mind to allow healing or to be happy?

As we have seen muscle testing from Applied Kinesiology can be a way of making the ego mind conscious. It is a way of tapping into your deeper inner wisdom and knowingness to determine what you honestly know to be true or false. It can get beyond the endless chatter in your mind and tell you whether you are being honest with yourself or whether you are unwittingly deceiving yourself.

If someone asked us, do you want to get well and continue to have a totally healthy life most of us would say, "of course!" as revealed in my little survey. Yet, as I described earlier, I was shocked in my polls to discover through muscle testing that virtually 100% of the time we all will find that our inner wisdom says the answer is that we don't deserve it or it's not safe *even though you consciously say that you do want to be well.* And these were only two of many barriers. But are you totally healthy and happy most of the time? The truth will be expressed in what is manifested in our bodies and in our lives. It is hard for us to remember that only about 5% or less of our behaviors are conscious, therefore more than 95% of our behaviors are unconsciously expressed in the mindbody. Muscle testing helps us get to the unconscious quickly.

But even if you many have doubts about the validity of muscle testing, I believe that you will discover that the answers you get from muscle testing tend to be highly consistent with what has been and is currently being manifested in your life. For example, if your muscle testing reveals that it is not safe or that you are not worthy of having total health and happiness, then you will most likely <u>not</u> be manifesting total health and happiness in your life in a consistent way.

But then, if we see how we helped to create our illness or unhappiness, the ego mind will most likely rush to make us feel guilty by judging ourselves for having followed its guidance. And to further complicate things for us, when we are not getting what we say we want, the ego mind offers another alternative: blame it on anything or anyone external rather than seeing it is connected to my inner truthful desire, often one that has been unconscious. And if we focus on it as happening to us from out there, then we will not look inside where we will find the true answer and can choose heaven instead of hell now. We get diagnostic labels placed on our bodies and our symptoms and external remedies to cure these labels. It may seem then that we have had a cure when the symptom is gone, but the true healing has not occurred, for we continue to view ourselves as separate and powerless, disowning our True Identity as immensely powerful. We are not fully healed just because the physical symptom is no longer present, unless the mind that needed the body to be sick has been healed as well.

And then the ego mind does even a worse thing. It will try to make us blame ourselves and feel guilty for being sick in order to keep us from just using our new consciousness and embracing our power of choice and being well. Guilt is always just the ego mind trying to keep us in suffering once again, for if we feel guilty we are more likely to repeat that which we feel guilty about! "Guilt is always insane and has no meaning," says *A Course in Miracles*. Muscle testing will help us get past the self deceptions which the ego mind always throws up for us.

Using Muscle Testing to Uncover Your Barriers

1. First, you must identify whether muscle testing is working accurately for you. I do this by simply asking the person being tested to extend his or her arm out to the side or toward me and to resist as I press down *firmly* on the arm *at the wrist area*. <u>Be sure to place and hold your hand on the wrist (not above it and not slapping down) before, during and after you press down,</u> otherwise you will not get adequate leverage, nor can you perceive the difference in strength. This way you determine the person's relative strength. (For a clear demonstration, you can download, free of charge, the video from my web site: www.henrygrayson.com).

2. I then ask a person to make a statement which we both know to be true, such as the person's accurate name vs. a false name, the accurate color of what they are wearing vs. a false color, accurate or false gender, the accurate day of the week and an inaccurate day, and so on. Invariably, the person's arm will become strong if the statement is true and will become weaker if the statement is false. This is true even when the person is trying hard to resist as much as she or he can on both the accurate and the inaccurate statements. It actually works when the person is trying even harder to resist on the inaccurate statement, because in spite of the greater resistance the arm goes weak. I have had strong men who work out with heavy weights daily in the gym tell me they tried as hard as they could to resist on the negative side, but their arms will flop down weakly, often pressing with only one finger.

If I do not get a clear distinction between the true and false statements, (1) I simply remind the person to "resist as much as you can," just before I press down on both the true and false statements. (2) Or you may need to press harder and more quickly on both the true and false statements. (3) Or a person may be dehydrated and will need a glass of water in order for it to work. Some people will have dramatic distinctions while others will be minor. The only thing necessary is that there is a noticeable distinction in comparative strength.

3. Next, we then move to statements where the truth may not be conscious to us, such as, "I want to get completely well right now!" vs. "I don't want to get well right now." Whichever statement one's inner wisdom knows to be the truth will make the arm strong upon resisting as we press down on it. And it will most likely be consistent with the degree of success or health the person is actually experiencing. In muscle testing, you do not ask questions. You make a true statement followed by the opposite false statement, and see which is stronger when you press on the person's arm.

If you have someone who can do muscle testing on you, test out the issues below: However, if you do not have someone to do muscle testing on you, there are ways to do these clearing processes without the use of muscle testing. I will describe these later.

What To Use the Muscle Testing For:

There are a variety of uses for muscle testing which can be very helpful in getting past our deceptive ego minds. Muscle testing helps us not lie to ourselves. The ego mind will often want us to think a negative belief or trauma is not present so we can ignore it and not clear it, then we can remain in the suffering, which it causes. It will also try to get us to think one is fully cleared when it is not, again so we will keep our suffering. Remember, the ego mind is the part of our mind which wants us to remain in pain, fear, and sickness instead of joy, peace, and health. We could try to figure out whether we have such traumas or beliefs for months by talking about them, and we are often still not accurate. Muscle testing helps us identify the problems much more quickly and accurately so we can do what it takes to be free of them.

1. You can use muscle testing to determine whether you have (a) a negative belief, (b) uncleared trauma, (c) a negative emotion, or (d) a negative download or identity.

2. Once you determine that one of the above exists, you can use muscle testing to ascertain the strength of disturbance of the trauma, the strength of the negative belief, negative emotion, or negative download or identity on a scale of 0-10. There are Check Lists of traumas and negative beliefs in later chapters to help you identify the ones you carry.

3. Muscle testing can also help you to determine when you have cleared any of these and brought them down to a zero, using any of the processes described in the next chapters.

4. You use muscle testing to determine the strength of a positive belief you are installing to replace the old negative one, also using the scale of 0-10 in order to make sure you keep doing the process until it is brought up to a "10".

5. You can use muscle testing to identify and then clear a negative energy reversal. A negative energy reversal is much like reversed energy in an electromagnet. If you put current in one direction, it will pick up

a junked auto and lift it onto a railroad car. If you reverse the energy it will release and repel the junked auto onto the railroad car.

Sometimes as little children, if we experienced intense traumas, considerable neglect, or were around pervasive negative energy, our basic energies could have gotten reversed. You can check for basic energy reversals by muscle testing the following true and false statements. If your arm becomes strong on any of the negative statements, you will need to use the EFTA (described in the next chapter) for bringing the negative energy reversal back into alignment in order to get the best results.

I deserve to be totally happy and healthy vs.
I don't deserve to be totally happy and healthy.

I am worthy of being totally happy and healthy vs.
I am not worthy of being totally happy and healthy.

It is safe for me to be totally happy and healthy vs.
It is not safe for me to be totally happy and healthy.

It's OK for me to let go of this part of my old identity vs.
I'm afraid of letting go of this part of my old identity.

You will need to use the EFTA to clear these Basic Energy Reversals which you discovered through muscle testing the items above. The EFTA is also demonstrated clearly so you can

follow along with it by downloading it free of charge from my web site: www.henrygrayson. com.

6. You can also use muscle testing to determine the accuracy of the answers you have to the other tools, including "My Six Questions" and the "Health and Attitude Awareness Questionnaire", as well as others which might come up in later chapters.

You may also use muscle testing:

(1) to confirm or disconfirm the traumas or negative beliefs you identify in the questionnaires in Chapters Four and Five, and
(2) to find the strength of their current negative influence on your health and life, or
(3) to determine if there are barriers in the way of your clearing your traumas or negative beliefs.

Muscle testing will confirm or disconfirm whether you are on the right track with your answers, getting the answers quickly, rather than having to speculate about them for a long time. It also helps us get past our self deceptions, so we can identify and clear what needs to be cleared for healing, health, and happiness. *Once the strength of each negative statement is determined, we will demonstrate (in the next chapter) how we can give a heightened focus of intention by using newer methods of acupressure point stimulation by touching these points and breathing or tapping on them, combined with bilateral stimulation of the brain.* We must remember that in this quantum and digital world, our beliefs and traumas are just information systems encoded in the energy systems of the mindbody. We can do the equivalent of pressing a delete button to clear this information.

Muscle Testing Guide to Determine
Very Early Origins of Illnesses

**(A printable PDF version of this is available on my web site
for your convenience: www.henrygrayson.com)**

List Your Illnesses or
Symptoms: _____

_____

_____

_____

_____

_____

Note: All phrases in "quotes" are to be stated aloud while muscle testing. If disturbances are revealed from any specific experiences or years, assess degree of disturbance on the 0-10 point scale. Do muscle testing as follows:

"There are uncleared traumas (painful experiences) which contribute to this illness"
"There are no uncleared traumas contributing to this illness"

If the arm was strong on "there are" then identify and test "when and what". _____

_____

Then test each possible painful event you have listed and rate it on the "0-10" point scale as to the amount of disturbance remaining with you.

"These occurred in (test to see which years produces a strong arm):

_____ "teenage years"

_____ "grammar school years"

_____ "pre-school years"

If the arm was stronger on any of the above (teenage, grammar or preschool), then test for specific years and degree of disturbance from each year.

Then test:

"There were intrauterine traumas contributing to this illness"

"There were no intrauterine traumas"

If the arm was stronger on "there were", assess degree of disturbance: _____

Then test:

"There were genetic memories contributing to this illness"

"There are no genetic memories contributing to this illness"

If the arm is stronger on "there are genetic memories" then test:

"There is one genetic memory"

"There are two genetic memories"

"There are three or more genetic memories", etc.

Then assess the degree of influence of each genetic memory affecting this illness or problem today on the scale of "0-10".

Then test:

"There are past life traumas contributing to this illness"
"There are no past life traumas contributing to this illness"

If the arm was stronger on "there are", ascertain how many past life traumas or which are contributing to this illness, as you did above with genetic memories. Rate them on a scale of 0-10. (The demonstration video of muscle testing is available for viewing or you can down load it from on my web site: www.henrygrayson.com, and this will make the process much clearer.)

Take Karen, who rarely exercised, ate unhealthily, and allowed a cascade of negative, worried, and victimized thoughts throughout the day, even though she said she really wanted to attend to all of them to help her be healthy and happy. We discovered that she had two basic energy reversals in place: "I don't deserve to have a totally healthy and happy life," and "I'm not worthy of having a totally healthy and happy life." The strength of each of these on a 0-10 point scale was a "10." Using the EFTA described in the next chapter to clear out these reversals, we were successful in bringing the strength of these beliefs down to a "0." Once cleared, Karen was able to allow herself to exercise and sleep in healthy ways, change her eating habits, as well as to be much more conscious of a choice about which thoughts are to linger in her mind. To deal with the eating problem effectively, however, there were a number of other issues which needed to be attended to.

<u>If you have no one to test your arm, just do the complete EFTA process on each of the above negative statements, treating them as if they are all true for you,</u> since most of us have some barriers to clearing our traumas, negative beliefs, negative emotions, and negative identities. You will use this shotgun approach, clearing a range of log jams in order to be certain that you have released any blocks which would interfere with your clearing exercises. Remember, these reversed energetic beliefs are most often not conscious to us, but are still affecting us. The proof is in the pudding, however, as we have seen. If you are not mostly and consistently healthy, joyous, and at peace, and if you have trouble consistently sustaining healthy lifestyle practices, then you most likely have one or more of these energetic blocks at work, and it would be best to clear them as soon as you come to the clearing processes described below. To do so will help you benefit much more from the various tools presented throughout this book.

CHAPTER 5

Uncleared Traumas: A Major Barrier to Health and Happiness

Be not the slave of your own past, plunge into the sublime seas, dive deep, and swim far, so you shall come back with self respect, with new power, with an advanced experience that shall explain and overlook the old.
Ralph Waldo Emerson

Much research and clinical evidence reveals that unresolved traumas play a very large role both in depression and in serious illnesses, thereby also bringing a high correlation between depression, ongoing anxiety, and physical illnesses. Multiple studies as well as clinical evidence shows that traumas, depression, and physical illnesses seem to be unmistakably intertwined, causing uncleared traumas to keep us slaves to our past.

Most people think of traumas as simply only catastrophic events which happen to some of us once or on rare occasions. I propose that we use the word traumas to encompass much more than these catastrophes. The insidious and ongoing painful experiences of childhood (and even adulthood) such as neglect, physical or emotional abandonment, continuous judgments, blame and criticisms, frequent yelling and anger, not being listened to, lack of support and encouragement, feelings not being acknowledged, lack of guidance on how to manage challenges—all as manifestations of a lack of love, safety, and positive attention—sometimes have much more of a deleterious effect on a child or adult than a single catastrophic trauma. These experiences can have a greater effect than the defined traumas of physical, verbal, or sexual abuse. All produce stress, which is a major factor in 80-85% of all our illnesses. *In fact, as noted earlier, numerous studies show that there is a very high correlation between unresolved childhood traumas and the onset of serious illness, both physical and emotional, often in early adulthood.*

Most of the medical and even much of the psychological professions have become convinced that depression comes from an imbalance of two brain chemicals, serotonin, and norepinephrine, and that the solution is to take a drug which is supposed to balance these neurochemicals. On the one hand, no research has conclusively pinpointed an exact or perfect amount of serotonin a person needs. More importantly, such a chemical solution to depression does not get to the cause of why the brain chemical imbalance is off to begin with, uncleared traumas being one extremely important cause, although not the only one.

For when traumas are not cleared, the survival brain gets hyperactive, secretes more adrenaline and cortisol, the stress hormones which deplete serotonin and create depression. Adult traumas, such as major accidents, the loss of loved ones, jobs, or significant possessions, break ups of marriages, ongoing marital conflict, crises with children, crime, significant financial strain, high-pressure bosses or dysfunctional work situations, can also traumatize a person enough to set him up for minor or major illnesses. In fact, the loss of any thing or person we are attached to can be experienced as a trauma as well. Invasive medical procedures such as surgery, anesthesia, invasive medical tests, hospitalizations, and sometimes even a diagnosis or negative prognosis may be traumatic enough to trigger the onset of another significant illness within a short span of time.

For example, a study done by Dr. Janice Kiecolt-Glaser at Ohio State University College of Medicine found that allergic responses to simple natural allergens can be heightened by a single instance of social stress. And allergic responses occur more frequently if the person had experiences that made him fearful or had parents who were fearful, seeing danger all around and thereby keeping the immune system overly reactive interpreting things as dangerous even they are innocuous. Major traumas can create a minor illness in as little as a few hours, while others, both major and minor may germinate for a few weeks to a year before manifesting as a significant symptom due to the prolonged secretion of stress hormones

Traumatic and disturbing experiences affect certain parts of the brain directly, with serious consequences. Such experiences, when not cleared (in ways we will describe later), can render the hippocampus inactive and even cause it to atrophy. The hippocampus is the part of the brain which normally interprets perceptions and puts events into a context and helps us to exercise control. But when the information of past pains or dangers has been encoded, when this part of the brain's activity is reduced, it sets us up for the amygdala (part of the survival brain) to react to seemingly insignificant events as if they were a danger of death itself. As a result, we then live our lives in a state of ongoing emergency. In such a state of existence, the blood is sent away from the prefrontal lobes, the rational part of the brain, directly to the deep limbic system, the survival brain, which puts us into survival mode constantly deciding among three, primal options: flight, fight, or shut down. At the same time blood is also taken away from the digestive system and sent to the arms and legs which are needed for fight or flight, resulting in important nutrients not being digested to keep the immune system strong. Is it any wonder that unreleased traumas would then reduce the immune response and then cause us to get sick, physically or emotionally? *Drugs may temporarily sedate the limbic disturbance, or balance the serotonin for temporarily stopping depression, but they do not clear out the effects of traumas, which are at the root of the problem.*

Imagine you are having a peaceful ride in a rowboat on the Niagara River, not knowing there is a waterfall below. You are relaxing, and enjoying the cruise you believe will help you heal an infection. Suddenly you hear the sound of the waterfalls, and instantly, your arms and legs go into motion, rowing furiously to get to the shore before you are thrown over the falls. It is good that the blood flowed to your arms and legs, for it helped to save your life. To fight the infection would be a moot point if you go over the falls; but what about that infection in your body at the same time? The immediate survival need dominated the need to digest nutrients in your stomach to strengthen your immune system. If you went over the waterfall, there would be no need to heal the infection. But as soon as you were safely on the shore and could relax again, the blood flow will go back to your stomach to do its work there to boost your immune system so your infection could heal.

On the other hand, if for some reason you were subjected to continual stress, your immune system would therefore continually be deprived of nutrients. You would have difficulty in healing and could be more likely to get even sicker. Biologist Bruce Lipton, former medical school professor, uses a wonderful analogy to describe this phenomenon. (See *The Wisdom of Your Cells* for an outstanding clear description of how your cells function in relation to consciousness). Consider the bomb shelters used during the cold war with the Soviet Union. When an alarm went off, everyone raced to bomb shelters immediately. Everything productive and growth enhancing in the community stopped: people left businesses, schools, factories, and stores. If they found that everything was safe from another signal in fifteen minutes, everyone would go back to their normal functioning without too much disturbance to their normal routines. However, what would happen if there was no signal that everything was safe and we continued to live in the fear of attack. How long could we survive in the bomb shelter without nutrients? Perhaps some items were stored there, but how long would they last? If they got no more nutrients, they would deplete their reserve, starve, become sick, and then die.

The equivalent happens to our immune systems. When the blood is drawn away from the stomach and digestion, our immune system weakens due to getting less and less nutrients, and we become sick or die. When we live in a state of continual stress, experiencing danger as lurking all about us, our immune system is not able to stay replenished. Therefore unresolved traumatic stress is a key factor in major illnesses such as heart disease, cancer, AIDS, multiple sclerosis, and others, as well as repeated minor illnesses such as colds, flus or back pains. When a child has been neglected or abused, had parents divorce, or taken away from their birth mothers, they are far more likely to use drugs and alcohol as they grow up. In addition, victims of violence may undergo long-term structural changes in their brains, particularly if these traumas are not cleared. The brain might even shrink. Traumas often will shut down the speech center (Broca's center) in the brain, which can make it more difficult for a child to tell someone about what happened to get protection, which then intensifies and locks in the trauma since the child remains in a state of vigilance, helplessness and danger.

A 1998 study by Vincent Felitti, M.D., et. al., reported in the Volume 14 of the *American Journal of Preventive Medicine* concluded that persons who had experienced four or more categories of childhood exposure (traumas) had 4-12 times the increased health risks for alcoholism, drug abuse, suicide and depression. They also found that the number of categories of adverse childhood traumas showed a graded relationship to the presence of adult diseases including heart disease, cancer, chronic lung disease, skeletal fractures, and liver disease.

Other studies have shown that victims of posttraumatic stress disorder (PTSD) have higher T-cell lymphocytes, and if chronic, are likely to be at risk for autoimmune diseases. It is as though they now attack themselves as they were attacked earlier in life. If we learned to be critical and attacking of ourselves, often beating ourselves up, we are more likely to develop an autoimmune disease, which is our immune system attacking our own bodies just as we are attacking ourselves emotionally. We might even attract more of the same kinds of painful experiences unless these traumas are cleared.

To look at a further and more dramatic picture, uncleared childhood traumas may not only set us up for the likelihood of serious illnesses in early adult life, but also make us less resilient throughout adult life when additional challenges or traumas come our way, making us more easily traumatized again as adults. For example, soldiers who are traumatized in a war have much more difficulty getting past such traumas if they also had experienced early childhood traumas. To truly help returning veterans, therefore, we need to assess and clear not only the strength of the war traumatization, but also assess whether any soldier had experienced childhood traumas which might have been reactivated as well, and clear that level too. Clearing out both levels of trauma must be done in order for the clearing to be effective, not only for veterans, but for all of us who have experienced both childhood and adult traumas.

Each type of trauma can be cleared quite effectively, simply, and often quickly—not as a way to pathologize the problems of soldiers but to treat war and re-entry as a trauma that necessarily needs to be cleared. Indeed, *clearing the effects of war, combat, or military training should be a part of the debriefing process for human beings having been at war and are now returning home.*

But traumas affecting our health do not only begin after we are born, but also occur even earlier in the uterus and during birth. They can also be attached to the first year of life, past life, or even what is speculated to be what I call a parallel life. We have also been able to help people heal who are suffering from genetic memory traumas. Let's take a look at these different types of traumas.

Intrauterine Traumas

Studies of babies in the uterus have been quite revealing. Very tiny cameras have been implanted in the uterus in order take pictures of the fetus when the mother is experiencing different situations. For example, if the parents are being loving or affectionate, having a pleasant conversation, or listen to melodic music such as Mozart, the fetus looks peaceful and happy and its little body is relaxed as well. If the parents are having a fight or the fetus hears acid rock music or rap, it will straighten up, back arched, and display distinct signs of extreme tension, as if trying to escape from the disturbance. These experiences cause the baby to receive stress hormones from the mother through the umbilical cord, feel the tension from her and the environment energetically, and then the information from these disturbing experiences is encoded in the little developing body and in the developing limbic system, the basic survival brain. This encoding can have significant influences on us after we are born, predisposing us to react more easily to similar disturbing experiences, the information for survival already having been downloaded into our limbic system. No wonder we do not understand where our reactions come from, since they are not only pre-memory, pre-language, but are often even pre-birth. I will show you later how these can be identified and cleared.

Birth Trauma

Otto Rank, M.D., a contemporary of Sigmund Freud, developed a theory of personality development based on the birth trauma, concluding that birth is a trauma for almost everyone. While some will have a difficult time getting out of the uterus, such as a breach birth, and have to be pulled out with forceps, or have the umbilical cord wrapped around the neck, others may find it traumatic to leave the soft, warm, protected environment and enter into the physically cold atmosphere, often needing to be spanked to start the breathing. Now hunger appears for the first time, wetness is uncomfortable, and physical closeness has been interrupted dramatically. Some babies will experience all this as traumatic and others will not, either way setting a tone for future experiences, positive and negative. Again, however, muscle testing from applied kinesiology can be used to identify if there is a birth trauma which is negatively influencing your life today. (See demonstration on video.)

First Year of Life Trauma

The first year of life after coming out of the uterus is one of the most important formative years in our lives. There are more new experiences and brain development than in most any other year. Eric Ericson, in *Childhood and Society*, referred to it as the year for developing a sense of basic trust versus mistrust, which profoundly influences the rest of our lives. We need consistency in having our basic needs met. But even more important is the need for a strong loving attitude and feeling on the part of our mother and other caretakers, combined with a lot of holding and interaction. If your mother, for example, was facing a trauma of her own when you were an infant, such as the loss of a parent, conflict with your father, severe economic stresses, or a feeling of being overwhelmed, she might not have been as capable of being present for you as you needed her to be. If your mother was unfortunately instructed by the pediatrician to let you cry when hungry and to feed you only by the clock, you probably felt much deprivation and also your mother's anxiety and guilt over following the doctor's instructions. Or what if you had to spend time in an incubator being totally separated from your mother? These traumas are simply downloaded in our little developing brain and other parts of the body. This is the year when much depression has its beginning, (see the work of John Bowlby), for it was the year in which we were totally helpless, not able to do much of anything on our own behalf and were totally dependent on consistent loving care from our caretakers.

It is extremely important that these traumas be cleared. You can use muscle testing to determine whether you had first-year-of-life traumas. But if you have no one to do muscle testing, you can do the TFT (Thought Field Therapy process below) to do the clearing on yourself or a loved one if you suspect at all that there were some first-year-of-life deprivations or traumas. No harm can be done, and there is much potential gain in doing the process, even if you have no such early traumas that you remember consciously.

Past Life Traumas

I do not know if past lives are a literal experience or if they are metaphors. There is literally only an eternal now, for past is gone and future is not yet here. Therefore they do not really exist. However, in this world of time and space we experience things as being in the past, even though it is only a memory. But for this work, it does not matter whether you believe past lives are literally true or whether you think of them as metaphorical, for both are just encoded information in the Unified Field of which we are a part. By accessing the field, combined with conscious intent, I find in my clinical experience that this encoded information can be released even without the past life traumas being remembered. Regressive hypnosis is not necessary.

Marilyn, for example, came to see me because of severe anxiety attacks. I used all the many different psychotherapy approaches I had been trained to do in my attempt to help her. Nothing was working. One day she entered her session saying, "Henry, I think these anxiety attacks originated in a past life. I cannot remember a time in my life that I ever felt peaceful. I have always felt anxious. Is there anything we can do about that?" I had just learned how to do muscle testing from applied kinesiology (AP) a short time before. I had never used muscle testing in this way, nor did I know anyone who had. Nevertheless, I ventured out by saying, "Let's do some muscle testing and see what your inner wisdom reveals." I asked her to extend her arm and resist me pushing down on it as I asked her to repeat each of the following statements:

My anxiety attacks originated in a past life.
My anxiety attacks did not originate in a past life.

Her arm became very strong when making the first statement, and fell weakly when making the second statement, telling us that indeed she was right. We tested it further and discovered that there were three past lives. Using the same process, which I describe below, we cleared out each of the three past life traumas and her anxiety attacks totally disappeared! We continued to work on other issues in her life, but she had become free of anxiety for the first time in her life.

One might ask, "How can this be? How can a problem be solved so quickly?" It is helpful to remember that clearing the effects of traumas can be best understood as being like deleting information which is outdated on your computer. As renowned physicist Erwin Schroedinger has noted: "The number of minds I have been able to observe in the universe is one." Perhaps it is the one mind of the Unified Field where the information is encoded that pertains to what we call past lives. As we do the equivalent of a wireless web search, we find just that information and release the emotional charge that makes it appear dangerous and threatening. I learned with Marilyn that she did not have to retrieve memories of this past life in order to release them. My experience with Marilyn opened up to me a whole new world of what is possible, in contrast to our old Newtonian world view where so much is thought of as impossible. Most people, however, do not get such drastic and complete results so quickly, for most problems have other "tentacles" which need to be attended to.

Remember, there are no traumas in our brains just as there are no words, no pictures, nor sounds in our computers, only encodings of information. When you type a command into your computer, your smart phone, you decipher pieces of information which appear as words or pictures on your screen. Perhaps the painful experiences of our past can be thought of as just encodings of information which can be deleted. We do not delete the memory, however, but we can delete the interpretation which creates the emotional charge on the memory which gets reactivated in the present situation by our ego minds.

Such a result would not be possible in the Newtonian world of cause and effect. But in the quantum world, we are not constricted so narrowly. Particles are popping in and out of existence constantly, basically as only tendencies to exist. We shape these tendencies by our consciousness, whether the vibrational level of energy slows down enough to be what we call matter, or whether it remains only as energy. We shape these outcomes through consciousness. Sometimes I like to think of this system in our mindbodies and the cell membranes which receive the information as being like good little soldiers. They are great at following orders. Unfortunately, many of the orders we have given our mindbodies have not been conscious and have been negative and limiting.

Parallel Life Traumas

One theory in the new physics is that there could be parallel universes, even existing in the same space, but at a different vibrational level, so that it is not visible to us in the earth's vibrational level. Within this theory, we could exist in one or more parallel lives, which could affect our lives here. Using muscle testing, I only occasionally find that there is a parallel life trauma affecting the person's health or other life problems today. I have also found that when it is discovered and then cleared, it usually makes a difference in the person's life.

In the ancient *Kabala*, they believed something similar to parallel universes. They believed that we lived on seven different planes at the same time, and that everything we thought, said and did on this plane affected our lives on the other six planes. Therefore they became very conscious of their thoughts, speech, and actions, so as not to adversely affect their other planes of existence. Not a bad idea!

I do not know whether parallel universes and therefore parallel lives are literal or not. Perhaps it could be a metaphor for accessing information in the unified field, and we are simply accessing it. But if doing a little muscle testing, doing a wireless web search in their minds, and then doing a three-minute process of stimulating some acupressure points and creating bilateral stimulation of the brain helps people to be free of some of their suffering, I am willing to do it. It has no harmful side effects, unlike most medications. Since I have found in my clinical experience that it works a very large percentage of the time, why would we want to refrain from doing it, even if some might think that something new and different is weird?

Genetic Memories: The Human Genome

Genetic memories are essentially encodings of information in our DNA from our ancestors who had to survive their challenges and traumas. Many are passed on to their offspring as a way of helping the species survive. They can be from a generation or two ago, or even hundreds of generations ago. Therefore, many times their experiences are not relevant to our lives here today, and instead of helping us adapt to our environment, the information may be counterproductive. The following is an example of how it can work in a productive way.

It was an early December day, quite cold, as it was almost the beginning of winter in New England. My family and I were driving around the shore to explore adjacent towns we had not become acquainted with since we had just moved to Connecticut. As we drove along the beach in one town, I spotted a tree full of parrots. I could hardly believe my eyes. What was a tree full of tropical birds doing in a tree on a cold New England day in this part of the world? As we kept driving we spotted another tree full of parrots as well and then a third tree! How could this be?

We began to ask people about this strange phenomena, and eventually found the story behind the parrots in New England. A few decades before a crate filled with parrots was being imported to the U.S. It was unloaded in the New York harbor, and loaded onto a truck to transport them to Boston. En-route, the truck had an accident, breaking open the crate and releasing all the parrots. Apparently, the birds migrated up the coast line of Connecticut, a number of them finding some kind of protective shelter to survive the winter. And as many creatures do, we pass on information we learned about survival to our offspring to help them survive, based on what we learned in our lifetime. So the offspring of these parrots knew how to survive the next winter and passed the information to future generations. Now there are flocks of parrots in various places on the coastline of Connecticut, surviving beautifully even in winter, for their genetic coding did not include migration.

We pass on such information in our genes which can go back for hundreds of generations! But although we pass on large amounts of information in our genes, only a certain amount of it gets activated, while other genes remain dormant unless they are activated later. Some are activated or deactivated even in the uterus. Some of this genetic information actually helps us survive. Squirrels know how to build nests high in trees that will withstand strong windstorms and protect them in the winter. Beavers know how to build dams with amazing skill which are strong enough to withstand immense pressure from tons of water. Much of the genetic information passed on to us is obviously quite helpful. On the other hand, let's imagine we had an ancestor who survived abuse in the concentration camps in Germany, or one many generations ago who found that the only way he received love was if he was sick, or one who almost froze to death in a Siberian winter, or one who lived through crises such as in Rwanda. What if these genes are activated, even though we are not in any circumstances which are similar to what our ancestors faced? We may not need their survival information; instead we may find ourselves over-reacting to current situations, but not understanding why, since that genetic information is not relevant to our now experience.

Suzanne had felt a deep sense of fear and dread all her life. She had been in several types of therapy at different times in her life and none had helped with this problem. After she came to consult with me, we carefully explored her childhood and family life, revealing nothing which would have contributed to such pervasive and ongoing fear. This led us to see the need to explore other origins.

Having been reading the findings from the research of a number of the world's top geneticists, I had discovered that the new conclusions were quite different than I had been taught in school. We were all taught that genes were pretty much etched in stone. If you had a certain piece of encoded information, you were quite likely to have it manifested in your life. Now the geneticists are saying that genes are quite changeable, and environment is one source of change, such as with the parrots in Connecticut. But environment may also include a factor which we have not previously thought was involved—consciousness. Here is where the discoveries from the quantum physics world view had begun to influence the thinking of geneticists, sparking the new field of epigenetics, (or epigenetic control) meaning that which is above the genes exercising control.

We know that cells have receptors on their membranes which receive various kinds of information. A common way a cell is influenced is by its material or chemical environment. But, as molecular biologist Bruce Lipton has pointed out, the cells are many, many times more responsive to the influence of energy and consciousness, perhaps 50 to 100 times more. Such a perspective could explain how sometimes there are fast, miraculous, and unexplained healings. It can also explain how we can influence the genetic predispositions in our lives.

I knew of one woman who was diagnosed with hypoglycemia, a pre-diabetic condition of low blood sugar, in her early twenties. Not only were both her parents diabetic, but all four of her grandparents. From a genetic standpoint, the odds of her becoming diabetic were clearly 100%. However, she followed a high protein/low carbohydrate diet, exercised regularly, and established a regular practice of meditation to reduce her stress level, totally believing that they would keep her from becoming diabetic. The last time I heard about her and her health, she was in her upper fifties and still had not become diabetic. How can this be? If we remember that everything in the universe is just information encoded in one large energetic field, then it seems that we might access that information in the unified field and even alter it, since we are part of it and none of us can ever separate ourselves from it.

But let us return to the story of Suzanne, who had lived with fear and dread all her life. Since I had learned that muscle testing from applied kinesiology can help us access some of the information in the unified field, I decided to do such testing with Suzanne. I first asked her to extend her arm and resist my pushing it down, in order to establish her relative strength. Then I asked her to make the statement:

"I have at least one genetic memory significantly contributing to this problem in my life."

As she made the statement, I pressed down on her arm, and found it to be quite strong. I then asked her to make the statement:

"There are no genetic memories significantly contributing to this problem in my life."

As she made the statement I pressed down on her arm and found it to be quite weak, indicating that there were indeed one or more genetic memories. I then asked her to state: "There is one genetic memory contributing to this problem today," and her arm became strong. "There are two or more genetic memories . . ." and again her arm was strong. "There are three genetic memories . . ." and her arm became even stronger. I then asked her to state: "There are four genetic memories influencing this problem," and her arm became weak. We then knew that there were three genetic memories which needed to be deactivated which were significantly contributing to her lifelong pervasive fears and anxieties. We did not know what her ancestors had experienced, nor what the specific information was that was passed on to her.

To delete the information encoded in these genetic memories, I decided to guide Suzanne through the Thought Field Therapy (developed by psychologist Roger Callahan, Ph.D.) which consists of stimulating several acupressure points by tapping on them, ones which Callahan found to be most helpful for clearing traumas, and then includes some exercises which increase bilateral stimulation of the brain. This is one of the earliest methods to use energy meridian stimulation, not by needles as in acupuncture, but by tapping on the acupoints for clearing traumas. I was not sure if it would also work for a genetic memory, but I knew from much experience that it worked to clear the effects of remembered traumas. Since it has no known harmful side effects, I decided to experiment with it to see if we could eradicate that DNA information which was not helping her survival, but was actually hurting her current life.

Since everything that exists is just energy and information encoded in the unified field, I instructed her to do the equivalent of a wireless web search, saying to her: "While holding your fingers on the forehead between the eye brows and slightly above them (a place which helps support focusing), take several slow deep breaths to relax . . . . Now, doing the equivalent of a wireless web search, instruct your mind to go to whatever place or places the information is encoded from the first of these three genetic memories— the information which is contributing to your pervasive fear problem throughout your life. Let your mind go there with the express purpose of releasing or deactivating that genetic information." I then guided her through the TFT process which is described below and is demonstrated more vividly in the videos. (*Remember, people find it much easier to understand these processes by watching a live presentation rather than* only *reading a written description, you may visit my web site:* www.henrygrayson.com *to watch or download the video demonstration.*)

At the end of the process she said that she had an image of being in a burning fire that Indians had set, and not being able to rescue other family members. While it is unusual for one to have scenes or memories connected with this process when it is prior to conscious memory time in this life, on rare occasions people will have images as Suzanne did. I do not know if the image was actually what her ancestors experienced or not, and it does not matter. It could be simply a symbolic representation of a fear-provoking trauma which an ancestor had experienced. Either way we are accessing the encoded information as in a web search, which I call genetic memories; for information from the past, in whatever form, is encoded in the unified field, and we are all part of that field of energy and information.

In any case, she was able to deactivate that genetic influence as well as the other two genetic memories, each with separate processes, for when we then did muscle testing we were delighted to find that the strength of the influence from that genetic memory was reduced from a "10" down to a "0". After these were completed, Suzanne said that she felt significant relief as she left the session.

More importantly, she began her session the next week by telling me with great excitement that she had never felt so peaceful as she had been since the previous session when we had completed deactivating the three identified genetic memories. In fact, she said, this past week is the most peaceful time with no fear that I have ever known in my entire life! I think the reason that the results were so dramatic and quick for Suzanne is that the genetic memories were the primary cause of her pervasive fear state, rather than diverse developmental experiences which most of us have.

Most of us have multiple causes, traumas in many different categories before and after we were born, and may not experience such extreme results so quickly. Our results will come when all the "tentacles to the octopus" have been dealt with. It's important to note, however, that in my several decades of clinical experience, I have found that neither such genetic memories nor our diverse traumas often do not seem to get cleared by talk therapy, as valuable as it may be for many other problems. And I have practiced, for decades, many forms of talking therapy, including psychoanalysis and cognitive therapy. Sometimes, brain scan studies show that talking about traumas can be rehearsing the story and reinforcing the problem by reactivating the limbic brain. To understand why such clearings work, we must continually remind ourselves of the new world view which promotes infinite possibilities for change. While the world seems to be made up of matter, it is pretty much entirely empty space and dancing energy responding to consciousness with just a tendency to exist. Such information can be deactivated much like deleting unwanted information in your computer.

When we have genetic memories that are adversely affecting our lives, ones which are contributing to our physio-emotional disturbances, they will tend to make us more susceptible to current painful experiences until cleared. They make us more sensitive to certain stimuli, or give more fearful interpretations to events happening in our lives. Or it may be that our mindbodies carry the programming to react in an unhealthy and non-adaptive way. And especially, this encoded information may take away our sense of free will and choice, which is just another way the ego mind may use the body and the material world for its purposes making us feel more powerless, little, and victimized in this illusion of separateness, thereby preparing the ground for more perceived trauma and sickness.

Certain South American shamans have known of this phenomenon for a long time, having been able to see the presence of this encoded information in the energy fields of people, telling them what illnesses they are predisposed to. They have their rituals for clearing out this information, which are supported by the strong beliefs of their tribal mind. It may be that various indigenous cultures have had the means to do what we are now just dis-covering through our scientific discoveries. Could it be that we are just uncovering what was there to be known all along?

If we should dis-cover that we do have genetic memories which are adversely affecting our lives today, then as we deactivate them, we will free ourselves of more barriers to total health, healing, and happiness. But not everyone seems to have such encoded genetic information, making their health more difficult, and most of us will also need to look through most of the other potential barriers to healing and happiness discussed in the chapters ahead for ones which we might be carrying. But since we know that we are no longer doomed by our genes, you can potentially deactivate the genetic memories which are not helpful to you with the TFT described below.

Getting to Our Unresolved Traumas

Psychological theorists from Sigmund Freud and Carl Jung to Eric Erikson have recognized that our personalities are largely formed by the time we reach school age. What an irony our human condition is! We are called upon to develop an operating system for our lives when we have no knowledge or experience in doing so. We may have minimal instruction, and even that may not be very effective or positive. So we draw conclusions the best we can at that age in order to survive as little children. And then we forget all but a handful of memories about our early-childhood experiences and the conclusions we drew from them as we formed our operating systems. We then find ourselves reacting and often over reacting to various situations, not at all understanding our reactions and wondering where they come from. Some may believe the cause is what happened in the present, not just the trigger. Others will conclude: That's just the way I am, not knowing how they got to be the way they are. And they do not know that these things are quite changeable often quickly. Nor do they know how to change this software or the operating system they created and then forgot. We need to make the unconscious conscious.

So many of our formative traumas, and therefore those contributing to our illnesses, are not in our conscious memory at all. Perhaps we were not held much as an infant, left alone crying in the crib for extended times even if we were uncomfortably wet, made to wait for food even when we were very hungry and occasionally some parents might have shaken us in frustration when we wouldn't stop crying.

Why is it that past painful experiences continue to influence us so much later on in our lives often many decades later? Using the PET, fMRI or SPECT scan for research, current brain scan studies show that when a person is either experiencing a painful experience or when the person is remembering and talking about a past painful experience, the survival brain, the limbic system, located just above the brain stem becomes alive with activity. Also, the person's adrenaline and other stress hormones elevate dramatically, the heart rate increases, and the galvanic skin response is increased. Why is the brain response the same with both an actual experience and a memory of such an experience? A trauma which remains as a memory is largely an encoding of information. The way the survival brain works is to set off a survival response when anything happens which is similar to the original painful experience. For example, one veteran who had returned from war was filling up his tank with gas at a service station. A car pulled into the next pump and backfired as the driver turned off the ignition. Hearing the loud noise of the backfiring, the veteran found himself under his car, having instantly thrown himself under it for protection as if he was still in the war zone. Needless to say, he was quite embarrassed to have others see him there. He was responding through eyes of the past, not from the present, which is what the limbic system does in all of us. It will literally act like a hijacker on an airplane, hijacking all rational functioning of the frontal lobes of the brain, as described by trauma researcher Bessel van der Kolk, M.D.

In our digital world, we can learn something about how our brains work. Knowing that the brain was the prototype of the modern day computer, we can look at the computer to get some ideas of how the brain works, although the brain is clearly far more complex. In your computer there are no words, no pictures, no music nor voices. There are encodings of digital information which need to be deciphered and presented on your screen. The same is true of our brains, other bodily cells, and energy systems. There are just encodings of information which remain from our traumas and other painful experiences. This information teaches the part of our brains called the limbic system how to interpret the signals which come into our bodies. If the cave man had been bitten by a rattlesnake, but managed to survive, there is an encoding of information which leads the limbic system to interpret anything resembling a rattlesnake as dangerous to survival. So, if he is walking in a forest at dusk and spots a dark, long cylindrical object, he may run away or look for a club to use to protect himself against the snake. He does not wait to see that it is just a piece of a dead limb which has fallen from the tree above.

We all do the same thing: any time something appears in our lives which we perceive as having a resemblance to our original source of danger, we react as if our survival is at stake. If the interpreted danger is somewhat pervasive in a situation, a location, a family, our work place, or on the street, we remain in the survival mode, constantly experiencing danger, keeping our survival brain over active, secreting the stress hormones cortisol and adrenaline relentlessly, therefore depleting our immune responses as well as sometimes damaging parts of our brains such as the hippocampus, leading to even further inaccurate analyses of danger. *For healing, health and happiness, these traumas need to be cleared so that the brain can restore itself to normal.* We must remember that only taking medicines will not get to this cause of illness, but will only treat the immediate symptom or emergency, sometimes creating other illnesses (side effects) while masking the real problem.

George, for example, had a father and mother who were highly critical, finding fault with so many things he did as a child. As an adult at work George found himself over reacting internally, if not externally, to his boss's simple suggestions as if they were major criticisms. Living with such perceived stress day after day kept him living in a survival mode and set him up for getting some kind of sickness as well as making him miserable, taking this joylessness home with him each night. Work then became not a place of joyful fulfillment, but a place of danger to him, taking blood away from his frontal lobes, making him literally dumber and less able to make intelligent decisions, also shutting down the speech center (Broca's center) so he could not speak up and talk it out satisfactorily. This situation stressed him even more and depleted his immune system so that he kept getting the flu several times each year. After ten years of living in this danger mode, it is no wonder that he was diagnosed as having cancer in the esophagus, an area needed for expression and speech. *Again, as well as removing the tumor from his throat, it was necessary that these traumas be cleared to be healed and remain healthy.*

As we have seen, the shifts in blood flow occurring in the brain and away from the stomach, the perception of danger creates a chain reaction of signals in which the amygdala releases cortisol and adrenaline. And if the perceived threat goes on and on, if not externally, then in our minds, we drain our immune systems. It is no wonder why some people, especially who have lived with ongoing perceived danger, producing traumatic stress, are diagnosed with adrenal deficiency. Trauma also raises the heart rate and disturbs the heart rate coherence, increases respiration, and shoots up the glucose level in the blood for fight or flight. Since these processes take so much energy, the cortisol tells other processes such as digestion, physical growth, and the immune system to shut down or slow down. When you are running from a tiger, it is more important to be able to flee than for your immune system to fight an infection. But when you continually perceive danger that is not there, or you feel you do not have effective tools for handling the external sources of stress, then you get depressed, continue to suffer from post-traumatic-stress disorder, and are more prone to heart disease, intestinal problems, gum disease, erectile dysfunction, diabetes and cancer. Chronic stress, including uncleared traumas, not only increases a rise in the stress hormones, but has also been shown to accelerate the growth of precancerous cells and tumors, and to lower the body's resistance to HIV and cancer-causing viruses.

I note the beginning of this same response in myself when I am pushing myself to work more quickly, such as getting bills paid and out of the way, or some other project. I will feel a bit tense, notice that my breathing is quick and shallow, and then check my pulse only to find that there was a lack of rhythmic coherence in my heart rate. I stop, breathe slowly and deeply for a couple of minutes, and let my heart return to its normal coherence. This demonstrates how easily our bodies are affected by perceived stress in the environment, and how quickly and easily we can bring back ease instead of moving further toward dis-ease.

More dramatically, Sylvia, at age 26, began to have anxiety attacks every time she saw the color red, a fire truck, a red coat in a store window, even a red light. When she was a child, she grew up with a mother who was a prostitute who entertained men in their apartment. One day, she heard frightening screams and sounds of beating coming from her mother's bedroom, then a man ran out of her room and raced away from the apartment. She went in to find her mother bludgeoned to death in a pool of red blood. The trigger for her repeated anxiety was the color red, representing the trauma of the loss of her mother, followed by the trauma of living in various foster homes where people only took in children for the money and did not give emotionally to her, which served to amplify the original trauma.

While most of us may not have had such dramatic traumas, we have other insidious, ongoing, painful developmental experiences, and all are significant contributors to our physical and emotional problems, disturbances in our relationships, and work failures. The encoded information can make images, sounds, words, and even certain gestures into a message which produces a reaction as if it was a trauma, even though it is not occurring now.

The new brain scan studies help reveal to us how the ego or false-self mind works to keep us in pain and in suffering. It uses the body and its encodings of past information to destroy the joy of the present and to project pain into the future. This part of our minds will do its best to keep us in suffering rather than in joy and happiness. No wonder it is hard for us to let our suffering go. Eckhart Tolle refers to it as feeding the pain body. The Russian philosopher Gurdjeif, as quoted earlier, recognized the human attachment to suffering thus:

You can call on human beings to make noble sacrifices for almost any worthy cause. But just don't ask them to give up their suffering!

And Sigmund Freud referred to it as the repetition compulsion. As we have seen from a spiritual perspective, as well as from the world view of quantum physics, it is an illusion that we are separate. It is the illusion of separateness which the illusory mind wants to keep in place. The part of our minds, which some call the ego, is simply an erroneous thought system in our minds which wants us to continue to think of ourselves as separate from our bodies, from others, from the earth, from the universe, and from the unified field, from our spiritual source, therefore keeping us separate from our true Power.

This illusory thought system makes us feel powerless and therefore experience ourselves as being acted upon, essentially as victims rather than creators, which in turn makes it easier to feel traumatized. It is the illusory ego mind, using the brain and other body parts to encode the painful information of our past traumas and other painful experiences, which keeps us away from joy, peace and health in the present moment by bringing in the pains of the past. Then it projects them into the future as well, which not only also destroys the joy of this now moment, but also destroys the joy of the future as well, since it is "the now" which creates the future. One neuroscientist told me that our reptilian survival brain is like Velcro to negative experiences and like Teflon to positive ones. This means that we must use a lot more positive psychological and spiritual practices to offset the reactions of the amygdala in our deep limbic system in order to stay at peace.

Reading such information about the massive accumulation of our traumas, plus those which are not remembered, is enough to make us depressed. "If they are not remembered, how can we ever clear them?" You might ask, "Is there any hope that I can be free of these determinants in my life in order to be happy and healthy?"

The answer is a resounding "Yes!" We are not going to re-cover them as in recovery. We are going to dis-cover them in a way that exposes the causes and clears them out with new and effective tools to get at the center of the traumas. While some of this clearing work has been done to a limited degree by regressive hypnosis, we will show you methods now which I find quicker and more efficient.

Thankfully, there are now available highly effective means of clearing out the effects of traumatic stress from the limbic system and other parts of the body. Some of these more complicated problems must be done with a skilled mental-health practitioner trained in these approaches, but there are some approaches which will be described later and demonstrated in the downloadable video that you can use on yourself, friends or family members as well as with a skilled professional. *However, If you have had a very intense trauma, it is usually better to clear it with a skilled psychotherapist who is trained in new trauma treatment methods, not just talk therapy, rather than doing it by yourself or with a friend.*

How to Identify Your Traumas

(A printable PDF version is available for your convenience on my web site: www.henrygrayson.com)

Place a check beside any of the traumas listed below which you think might possibly be unresolved or you think might still be affecting your life and health adversely today.

1. Losses by Death

____ parent

____ sibling

____ child

____ other close family member

____ divorce

____ spouse or partner

____ close friend

____ close caretaker

____ pet

____ other

2. Other Losses

____ friend

____ position

____ home

____ *health*

____ *valued possession*

____ *lover*

____ *accident*

____ job

____ money

____ child (children)

____ *family*

____ *partner*

____ *special caretaker*

____ *body function*

____ *other*

3. Singular Dramatic Traumas

____ *surgery*

____ *diagnosis or prognosis*

____ *anesthesia*

____ *abusive treatment*

____ *rape*

____ *terrorist attack*

____ *crime victim or witness*

____ *hospital stay*

___ spouse or partner had affair

___ neglected

___ divorce or divorce proceedings

___ other

4. Developmental Traumas

___ parent often angry

___ parents fighting verbally

___ physical abuse

___ criticized or judged

___ pressured to achieve

___ ignored

___ over protected

___ parent severely negative

___ parents overly involved

___ drug addicted parent

___ rarely given guidance or instruction

___ treated poorly by siblings

___ parents undependable

___ very lonely childhood

___ maltreated by teacher

___ parents too lenient

___ lack of love

___ no affection

___ not listened to

___ parents fighting physically

___ sexual abuse

___ parents threatening you or each other

___ shamed

___ parent alcoholic

___ parents uninvolved

___ parents frequently fearful

___ rage-aholic parent

___ emotional abandonment

___ got attention only when sick

___ not protected from abusive family members

___ got attention only when acting out

___ victim of bullying

___ caretakers overly strict

___ feelings not heard or respected

___ parents never expressed emotion

___ mentally ill or disturbed parent

others: _____

_____

_____   _____

_____

ON EACH CHECKED ITEM, ASSESS the amount of disturbance still with you and affecting your life today adversely.

Use a 10 point scale, "0" meaning no disturbance and "10" is a maximum disturbance. Use muscle testing, if possible, to make this assessment accurately. If muscle testing is not available, rate yourself as honestly as possible, thinking of how much that particular issue is still present in your current life experience. It is particularly noticeable if that issue is often present, recurring, or brings a strong emotional charge.

Place the number beside each trauma checked.

Techniques for clearing the effects of traumas are presented below and are demonstrated in video format which you can watch or download by visiting my web site: www.henrygrayson.com, where you can follow along with them to do your own clearings.

HOW TO IDENTIFY ANY UNREMEMBERED OR UNCONSCIOUS TRAUMA (as described in Chapter 4) Use muscle testing on each of the following statements. Remember to resist as much as you can each time.

TO REVIEW

1. GENETIC MEMORIES

There are genetic memories contributing to this problem today. (Test)
There are no genetic memories.
(Test)
If the arm was strong on "There are" then do the following:

There is one genetic memory contributing to this problem today. (Test)
There are two genetic memories contributing to this problem today. (Test)
There are three genetic memories contributing to this problem today. (Test)
Note where the arm became strong on these, and you will have your answer as to the number you will need to clear.

2. PAST LIFE TRAUMAS

There are past life traumas contributing to this problem in my life today.
There are no past life traumas contributing to this problem.

If the arm became strong on "There are" past life traumas then test:

There is only one past life trauma.

There are two past life traumas.

There are three past life traumas, etc.

The one on which the arm becomes strong is the number of past life traumas you must clear.

3. **ALSO TEST FOR:**
   INTRAUTERINE TRAUMAS
   BIRTH TRAUMA
   FIRST YEAR OF LIFE TRAUMAS

There are intrauterine traumas, (or birth traumas, or 1st year of life traumas) contributing to this problem today. (Test)

There is no intrauterine trauma (or birth trauma, or 1st year of life traumas) contributing to this problem today. (Test)

There is only one . . .

There are two . . .

There are three . . .

The number when the arm becomes stronger is the accurate one.

PREPARATION FOR CLEARING PRE-VERBAL TRAUMAS:

Thymus Heart Rub (to get rid of any barriers to clearing)

This is an especially effective tool for preparing yourself to clear traumas, making sure that you remove any barriers to letting the effects of the trauma go. (You may watch a video demonstration of the Thymus Heart Rub by visiting my web site: www.henrygrayson.com).

Bring your right hand to upper center chest and place it flatly over the thymus gland and rub soothingly in a clockwise (looking on from the outside) direction, while saying:

> I deeply love and accept myself even if I don't deserve to be free of this trauma.
> I deeply love and accept myself even though it's not safe to let go of this trauma.
> I deeply love and accept myself even if I'm not worthy of being free of this trauma.
> I deeply love and accept myself even if I'm afraid of letting go of this part of my old identity.

There are a number of reasons that the Thymus/Heart Rub is so valuable. First, the words: I deeply love and accept myself even though I don't deserve or it's not safe, or I am not worthy. This means that you have not suppressed or repressed the trauma or the blocks to clearing it, but have identified them. Next, you are stimulating the thymus gland, which produces T-cells in the immune system. You are also stimulating the energy of the heart meridian and the heart chakra. In addition, you are giving a soothing gesture to your body, taking your full hand, not just the fingers, to gently rub your upper chest in a deeply soothing and nurturing way.

Most of us have never learned constructive ways to sooth ourselves when disturbed, Instead we have turned to multiple addictions food, alcohol, drugs (illegal and legal), internet, TV, work, sex, tobacco, and others, making us the most addicted nation in the history of mankind! All of these as addictions are expressions of seeking for a solution outside ourselves and cause us serious problems of mind, body, and relationships. Why not use something like the Thymus/Heart Rub, which has no harmful results, but only aids in the healing of that disturbing emotion?

Gautama, who became the Buddha, stated it beautifully: "You yourself, as much as anybody in the entire universe, deserve your love and affection."

The TFT (A process from Thought Field Therapy effective for clearing preverbal traumas):

Use this clearing process for all traumas that occurred before you had language, including genetic memories, past life traumas, parallel life traumas, intrauterine traumas, birth traumas, and first year of life traumas.

(Start-Up:) Determine the amount of disturbance that is with you on a "10" point scale, using muscle testing, if possible (The video for demonstration of the Muscle Testing Tool is available to watch on my web site: www. henrygrayson.com). If someone is not available to assist you in muscle testing, try to guess the level of your disturbance as accurately as you can.

0	1	2	3	4	5	6	7	8	9	10
No disturbance					Moderate			Great disturbance		

This process consists of manual stimulation of certain acupressure points by simply tapping on or holding your fingers firmly on the acupoints. These points are taken from the ancient Chinese system of acupuncture, but you will tap on these points, (or hold your fingers on them while breathing) instead of inserting needles. In this ancient system, each acupressure point stimulates an energy meridian which runs through the body and is connected to an internal organ which symbolizes or is connected to different emotions, both positive and negative. When you stimulate the meridian to release a negative emotion, the positive naturally begins to emerge in its place. We used to think that such energy meridians were imagined or metaphorical, but now with newer technology they can be photographed, showing their existence.

Also, using an unusual ritual helps to give an increased focus of conscious intention, which is a central part of making this process work along with the stimulating of the energy meridians. Therefore, I think of this process as a ritual to create a more heightened focus of intention than we would normally have when we just think or talk about something. We then add an energy boost with the acupoint stimulation. When we remember that the body is just energy with tendencies to exist effected by consciousness, then it makes sense that such a process could be powerfully effective, not so much from a Newtonian perspective, but from a quantum physics and spiritual perspective.

THE TFT PROCESS (For clearing traumas before we had language):

Place your fingers on the center of your forehead, just slightly between and above the eyebrows.
Take several slow and deep breaths to relax.
Instruct your mind to do the equivalent of a wireless web search and to go to those places where the information to do with this preverbal trauma (past life, genetic memory, intrauterine, etc.) is encoded, and go there for the purpose of releasing it. Then tap quickly with moderate vigor:

Tap on the eyebrow next to the nose. (about 20 times)

Tap on the bone under the eye. (about 20 times)

Tap under the arm about 4 inches under the armpit. (about 20 times)

Tap on the collarbone about where a button down shirt collar would be, on the bone and slightly below it (about 20 times)

Tap on the GAMUT spot (on the back of the opposite hand between the little finger and ring finger continuously while doing all the following:

Tap with eyes closed.
Tap with eyes open.
Look down to the right.
Look down to the left.

Make a big wide circle all the way around with your eyes.
Circle your eyes back the opposite direction.
Hum a few notes of any tune
Count to five
Hum a few more notes
Count backwards from five to one.

Tap again on the inside edge of the eyebrow (about 15-20 times)

Tap on the bone under the eye (about 15-20 times)

Tap under the arm (about 15-20 times)

Tap on the collar bone (about 15-20 times)

Tap on the GAMUT spot again while looking down to the floor, and then slowly roll your eyes up toward the ceiling and try to look at your eyebrows (a minute or two)

Repeat this process until you have cleared all signs of the trauma OR you determine that your disturbance level is "0" on the "10" point scale.

PROCESS FOR CLEARING TRAUMAS OCCURRING <u>AFTER</u> YOU HAVE LANGUAGE

The EFTA (An adaptation of the EFT). The Emotional Freedom Technique (EFT) grew out Thought Field Therapy, the early work of psychologist Roger Callahan, Ph.D. One of his algorithms for traumas was described above. His approach was then simplified from many diverse algorithms to one simple approach by Gary Craig into the Emotional Freedom Technique (EFT). I have made an adaptation from the EFT which I find especially effective for (1) clearing traumas once we have language, (2) clearing negative beliefs which grew out of the traumas, (3) negative emotions, and (4) negative identities or downloads which we live by. As soon as we can speak and have more symbolic thought and mental processes, we are more likely to attach to our traumas. The ego mind has convinced us that there is some safety or other value in keeping it. The EFTA clearing process will work more effectively if we make sure there are no blocks to clearing the trauma (or belief, identity, etc.) It is also the process which people in ongoing therapy select most, using muscle testing.

PREPARATION FOR CLEARINGS (when you do not have someone to do muscle testing):

Before doing the EFTA process for clearing (trauma, negative belief, negative emotion, negative identity, negative downloads from parents), it is important to clear out any blocks to clearing them. It is much like clearing a log jam from a stream so that it can flow more easily. To do so, use the Thymus/Heart Rub described previously while repeating the following as you rub your upper chest in a clockwise circle (looking on from the outside):

"I deeply love and accept myself even if I might not deserve to be free of this problem."

"I deeply love and accept myself even if it's not safe to be free of this problem."

"I deeply love and accept myself even if I might not be worthy of being free of this problem."

"I deeply love and accept myself even if I'm afraid of letting go of this part of my old identity."

Now you are ready to do the process for clearing "after you had language":

THE EFTA

An Adaptation of the Emotional Freedom Techniques by Henry Grayson, Ph.D.

(You may watch a video demonstration of The EFTA on my web site: www.henrygrayson.com, and use it to follow for your clearings.)

1. **THE SET UP**:

   Place your fingers on your forehead in the center between the eyebrows.

   Take several deep breaths to relax, and then focus on your trauma.

   Allow any memories or scenes that represent this trauma to come into your consciousness.

   Notice what emotions come up with these memories. And then notice where you feel these emotions in your body. Focus on that place or those places.

Then with the full and clear conscious intent to release this trauma proceed with the process below.

2. Place your fingers on the eyebrow (next to nose), and say:
I now release all fear related to this trauma
Take several slow deep breaths.

3. Place your fingers on the outside edge of the eye and say:
I now release all anger, resentment and rage related to this trauma.
Take several slow deep breaths.

4. Place your fingers on the bone underneath the eye and say:
I now release all anxiety related to this trauma. Take several slow deep breaths.

5. Place your fingers on the upper lip under the nose and say:
I now release all embarrassment related to this trauma. Take several slow deep breaths.

6. Place your fingers underneath the bottom lip and say:
I now release all guilt and shame related to this trauma. Take several slow deep breaths.

7. Place your fingers under the arm, about 4 inches beneath the armpit and say:

I now release all worry and excessive concern related to this trauma. Take several slow deep breaths.

8. Place the fingers of both hands under the rib case directly under the nipples and say: I now release all hurt and sadness related to this trauma. Take several slow deep breaths.

9. Place your hand over the upper central part of the chest and:
   Imagine you are breathing love into your heart, and exhaling fear down through your solar plexus, as you take a number of slow deep breaths.
   (or you might remember a scene in which you felt a purity of love toward someone or from someone.)

10. Place your fingers on the collar bone, about where a button down collar would be, touching the bone and slightly below it, and take two or three slow deep breaths.

Many while find it quite helpful to use the video which you can view on www.henrygrayson.com to guide you through this process as you do your clearings. In fact, most people will find it much easier than using this printed version of the process.

EFTA Acupressure Points

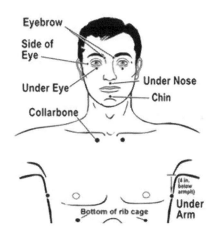

ASSESS THE STRENGTH OF DISTURBANCE FROM THIS TRAUMA (BELIEF, NEGATIVE IDENTITY) ON THE 10 POINT SCALE ONCE YOU HAVE FINISHED EACH EFTA CLEARING.

If you have someone to do muscle testing with you, determine whether the strength of trauma (belief, identity, download or emotion, etc.) is now down to a "0". If it is higher than a "0", keep repeating the process until you reach a "0". *If you can't do muscle testing* then DO THE EFTA PROCESS AT LEAST 3 TIMES TO BE SURE THAT THE TRAUMA (OR BELIEF OR NEGATIVE IDENTITY) IS CLEARED. It is cleared if the strength of the belief is down to a "0" on a "10" point scale. It is best to assess with muscle testing since it helps to get past our self deception, but if you can't, then do your own subjective rating and be sure you deeply know it is down to a "0" before you stop repeating the above process.

0	1	2	3	4	5	6	7	8	9	10

No disturbance   Moderate   Great

Go back through your list of traumas, and find the ones you have checked. Do this EFTA process systematically on each of them in order to make sure that you are not carrying that baggage with you. Use the video demonstrations to guide you through the process.

I think of each uncleared trauma we have as like walking up the hill of life with a backpack. With each disturbing experience or trauma which is not cleared, it is like adding a chunk of lead to your backpack. Before long, your backpack becomes heavier and heavier, and your mind/body begins to break down. It becomes increasingly difficult to keep hiking up the hill of life. However, with each trauma you clear, I think of it as taking a chunk of lead and tossing it aside, so your load gets lighter and lighter—hence more health, peace and happiness.

We Need to Clear All Our Past Traumas as they are retained in our bodies until released:

Dangers of Uncleared traumas:

Reduce our immune response

Help to make us sick

Make us depressed
Make us anxious

Increase and continue limbic and knee-jerk responses

Causes replays of old painful patterns in relationships

Set us up for irrational behaviors and reactions

Makes us dumber

Interferes with our happiness in mind and body

Benefits of Cleared traumas:

Thought monitoring easier

Easier to let go of negative beliefs

Easier to see another's person's perspective with compassion

Easier to forgive

Makes our immune system work more effectively

Makes us calmer

Decreases limbic and knee-jerk responses

Makes us smarter, more aware, conscious and present

Creates happiness in mind and body

Now we will turn to identifying the negative beliefs which are the conclusions we have drawn about ourselves and life as a result of the traumas we have had. Such conclusions serve to form a kind of "software" which we live by, until we identify and clear them. If we do not do this, we continue to let our lives and bodies be run by our old, but unwanted and outmoded software.

Chapter 6

Beliefs That Make Us
Sick . . . Or Well

It is your faith that made you whole.
Jesus of Nazareth

Our negative beliefs can make us sick—or at least unhappy. We have all heard the statement, once bitten, twice shy. While our ancestors sensed some kind of connection between a painful experience and our avoidance of others like them, we have discovered so much more since. It is more likely to be 15-18 times shy, since the limbic system is like velcro to painful experiences. From neuropsychology we have learned that the information of the trauma is encoded information in the part of the survival brain called the hypothalamus, which translates information to make us feel endangered and frightened, or to feel safe and secure. It may be encoded in other parts of the body as well. These painful experiences lead us to draw conclusions which gel into a negative belief, it grows out of increasingly imbedded information based on what is most dramatic or ongoingly familiar to a person, and is recorded in this part of our limbic system, much like software programming, making us interpret things as safe or unsafe, negative or positive, and react accordingly. This cumulative information can be from repeated negative experiences, leading to negative conclusions about our selves, about others, and about life. The accumulation of positive experiences would lead us to form more positive beliefs about ourselves, about others, and about life.

Our negative core beliefs, therefore, are the eventual conclusions we drew primarily from the negative and painful experiences, or traumas, of childhood. Such beliefs may grow out of unresolved traumas, repeated negative experiences, or even repeated negative thoughts associated with the painful experiences. In this sense, negative core beliefs are simply congealed thought patterns which have grown out of our traumas, the information encoded in the deep limbic system for survival, and overall conclusions we have drawn from them. Other beliefs are ones we have picked up from our families, communities, religious groups, news media, advertising, and all aspects of the world about us. Hence, many of our barriers to healing and happiness lie in our uncleared traumas, negative beliefs and repetitive negative thought patterns which are intertwined together, all of which must be attended to. All of these are simply encodings of information which literally becomes like software which will print out only what is in the program, unless it is changed or re-written.

Kenneth, for example, grew up in a family where both parents were totally negative about everything, yelling constantly. Virtually all of his parents' communications were critical of him or compared him negatively with someone else. Somehow, very early in life, he managed to view his parents as crazy. His solution was to stay away from them as much as he could by playing outside or going to play or read in his room with the door closed. As a result he maintained more of his self confidence and worth, did well in school going through college and medical school successfully and continued to remain physically healthy throughout his adult life.

On the other hand, Joan's mother would slap her around, lock her out of the house, and scream at her for every little thing. Other times she could be warm and playful. Joan grew up concluding that she was not loveable, did not deserve happiness and was not worthy of success, and if she did have it, she believed it would be snatched away easily and quickly. Unlike Kenneth, she did what most children do, concluded that something was wrong with her. As a result she was more traumatized, got into drugs for a period of time, and then had a variety of significant illnesses starting at age 21. Only after clearing her vast amount of traumas and negative core beliefs in her early forties did her health improve significantly.

We do not know all of what went into making it possible for Kenneth to see his parents as crazy and feel more control, while Joan concluded that something was wrong with her. Like Joan, some negative beliefs may come more directly from unresolved traumas and the immediate conclusions which were drawn from those experiences, or an accumulation of experiences. Yet other beliefs, negative and positive, may be simply absorbed in early childhood from those around us, much like downloading information into our computers. How does this work?

When we want to help someone reach a state of high suggestibility we will teach a person how to enter into a deep hypnotic trance state where their brain waves become slower and slower. In such a state they are much more receptive to the suggestions which they wish to have implanted. As small children, we are already in such a state.

When we are first born, and through the first couple of years, we are in Delta brain waves, the very slowest. Then for the remainder of the preschool years, we are in Theta brain waves, the second slowest. These preschool years are the period of time where personality developmental theorists say we form our personalities. Through the grammar school years, we are in Alpha brain waves, which is equivalent to a light to moderate hypnotic trance state. Only with the onset of puberty do we move into Beta brain waves, our most active. When we hypnotize someone to plant a suggestion, such as "you cannot tolerate the taste of cigarette smoke," the hypnotic induction is designed to slow down the brain waves to alpha or theta. Here the person is far more suggestible and the process is more likely to work. If we are already in these slow brain wave states, as in early childhood, we literally download everything around us without even thinking about it. And then, on top of our "downloads" we react to negative or positive messages we are given, and draw conclusions from the ways we are treated.

Since we are little and our parents are giants, we perceive them as gods who can do anything and know everything. Hence, if they treat us shabbily, abuse us, neglect us, don't give us enough love, attention and encouragement, we take it as our fault or deficiency. Our negative core beliefs emerge out of our negative conclusions about ourselves, people, and the world, doing the best we know how as little children.

As little children, we also. literally absorb or download everything around us—what we see, hear, taste, smell and feel. It is not so much the instructions or lessons we are taught, as an absorption of everything happening around us, including our parents' thought patterns, beliefs, attitudes, emotional states, behaviors, relational patterns and their ways of dealing with conflict and frustration. Our only freedom at that time is in how we interpret those experiences, and a common interpretation of the negative experience is that "I am not deserving or worthy." We erroneously come to the conclusion that something is essentially wrong with us. We view our parents as gods, capable of everything, so if we are not loved enough, we come to the conclusion that we are somehow deficient.

Our Negative Beliefs Help Create Sickness

Most obviously, negative beliefs which foster self criticisms, judgments, fearful reactions to the world, guilt, and feelings of inadequacy, all increase the flow of stress hormones which decrease the immune response. The effects of traumas and negative beliefs most often go hand in hand. We also typically download the beliefs, behaviors, and attitudes of our parents or other significant people in our lives, such as who gets sick, how they get sick, what makes you well, how people age, what is possible or not possible to heal. We might even conclude we must get the same illnesses as our parents and that we will die at the age they did. Other beliefs might be about what is possible or impossible to do about health or healing, whether we are worthy or deserving, and what is safe or dangerous. If a parent exclaims, "Don't put that dirty thing in your mouth. It will make you sick," then, if we turn it into a belief which we carry into adulthood, we are more prone to believe that since we were exposed to someone carrying a bacteria, we will probably get sick, and then we most likely will. (If we have uncleared traumas, this will also help make it so.) The physical fact is, however, if we don't put enough dirty things in our mouths as children, we may develop a much weaker immune system. In contrast to such a belief, however, I have learned over the years that I either allow or invite in a microbe (bacteria or virus) only when I have a need to get sick and have not identified the need and made other choices about that need.

While some of our negative beliefs are directly and obviously related to sickness and health, others do not appear on the surface to be related. However, they all create negative energy which weakens the mindbody through destroying our happiness, which makes all the body's cells unhappy as well. This is easily demonstrated: If you have someone who is focusing on a negative belief they hold, regardless of what it is about, have them extend their arm and resist your pushing it down, the arm will fall down very easily. Sometimes you might even be able to push it down with one finger even if they are resisting strongly. On the other hand, if you have them focus on a positive belief about themselves, about others or about life, when they extend their arm and resist, you will find the arm to be quite strong by comparison.

The implications of this little experiment are vast. If we are dwelling on thoughts which rehearse our negative beliefs throughout the day, regardless of what area of our lives, how much are we weakening every part of our mindbodies? What are we doing to our moods and our feelings? How do they cumulatively affect our cells and our immune response? How are they affecting everything we do, including how we relate to others, perform tasks at work, or play a sport? How does it affect the energy we send out and what we attract back? But most importantly, we are weakening our mindbodies continually in each moment we harbor such beliefs. No wonder our bodies eventually break down into a vast array of physical symptoms! Is it any wonder that optimists, those who have more positive belief systems, live longer? Research shows that pessimists may have a more accurate observation of the facts about them, but optimists not only live longer, but are also healthier and happier. It is hardly a coincidence that happy thoughts and beliefs make happy cells which typically result in a longer and healthier life. *Our thoughts and beliefs are acts of creation.*

The Dynamics of Our Beliefs

Our beliefs are largely congealed thought systems which then in turn fuel the chatter in our minds throughout the day. Then this continual chatter rehearses and reinforces our belief system, making it stronger and more deeply embedded. Even if we are presented with opposing information to counter that belief system, we may hang on to the old belief even more tenaciously, especially if it is one we are invested in, as social psychologist Leon Festinger discovered in his classic research on disconfirmation of beliefs in the middle of the 20th century. What a set up for failure or success! Our false self, our ego mind, is so insidious in its ploys, keeping us in patterns which will create more harm than good, and oppose our health and happiness, but only if we let it.

The good news is that the ego mind is only a thought system in our heads. It has no power at all except that which we give to it by listening to it and believing it. Ceasing to listen to and believe it is much like pulling the plug on its power source. While it is very helpful and ultimately necessary to monitor these negative thoughts, as we will see later, it may be difficult for some people to do. This difficulty seems to arise (1) from the fact that we have traumas which are not cleared, as discussed in the last chapter, (2) from the fact that the negative beliefs have not been cleared, and (3) and from those deeply entrenched beliefs and traumas which have reversed our basic energy. Clearing all of these impediments will help make it easier to be in charge of our thoughts, which is our ongoing necessity for health, healing and happiness.

As noted above, the beliefs we carry work much like software in a computer. Our computer will only print out only whatever the program we are using is designed to do. Similarly, if we are carrying a negative belief, then our internal software will be printing out that conclusion in our lives regarding our success, health, happiness, or relationships. If we clear out the effects of our traumas and the old software of our negative beliefs, then we will be better able to stop our negative thoughts, thereby ceasing to reinforce our beliefs with our constant internal chatter.

Can you imagine trying to stop a train by applying the brakes while several diesel engines are still powerfully chugging away to keep pushing it forward? Much like what we do, the train would be fighting against it self. And that fighting against ourselves burns up much needed energy, literally exhausts us, and makes us dumber in the process. When the cells in our bodies are continually exhausted and worn down, how could we not but get sick, anxious, or depressed? How could we not but fail in our tasks or in our relationships? Genuine high energy comes from having the bound up energy freed from unresolved traumas and beliefs and then changing our thoughts as well so as not to rebuild or reactivate them.

In our computers, when we delete an old outmoded piece of software, we usually desire to install an updated version or a newly designed program. We need to do the same with our old software, our negative beliefs. Once they have been cleared, using one of the tools you will find described later and demonstrated in the video, we need to install the new belief, our new software which we would prefer to live by at this point in our lives. We wrote our old software and our basic operating systems when we were tiny and did not have the slightest idea about how to do it. Now, do we wish to live our lives using an operating system designed by a one, three, or five-year old? Who of us would go up to a little three year old and ask him how to run our lives? In essence, we are often doing this automatically with our own inner three year old. Now is the time to write a new program designed for this place, time, circumstance, and age in our lives in order to be happy and healthy.

Are You Tired of What Your Negative Beliefs Are Creating?

Hopefully, we have learned a lot by this time in our lives about what does not work for us to keep us happy and healthy. We have seen so many of the guidelines or solutions presented by the ego mind lead us astray or worse, into suffering, using the childhood encodings of information. We now have the opportunity to cast out the old, which we do not want any more, and put in the new, which we now prefer. If there is anything that is a continuation in our lives, the manifesting of something we do not like or want, the odds are great that there is a negative belief we are carrying as our internal software. The adage, "the proof is in the pudding" is nowhere more relevant than in these real-life situations.

For example, Jamie had concluded from her childhood experiences of rejection by her mother and her father that she was always going to be rejected by anyone she had made important in her life, whether a boyfriend, a boss or a friend. Carrying this belief, I will inevitably be rejected, she would attract confirmation of it, leading to repeated rejections, over and over and over.

When we have a belief, negative or positive, we will do everything possible to get confirmation of that belief. As with Jamie, she would attract people into her life and chose to get involved with those who would be most likely to be rejecting of her. If this did not work, she, like all of us, would behave in a manner which would get the other person to be rejecting. She, again like all of us, would also send forth a magnetic force field to stimulate or attract that rejecting behavior from the other person. And if those two options do not work, we always have a third one, a back up measure, which will always work for us: *We will see others as being that way* (for Jamie it was rejecting) *even if they are not!*

But Jamie's belief did not stop with "I will inevitably be rejected." It went further and deeper to: "I am rejectable." So, each time she had confirmation of her belief that she would be rejected, she concluded even more deeply, saying to herself, "See, you really are rejectable!" And then, "if I am rejectable, I must be unworthy! Something must be wrong with me! Maybe I don't deserve to live!" The way the egoic mind works is that badness and wrongness deserve punishment. Guilt demands punishment. What better way to punish one's self than to get sick? Can we not see that it would be much easier for her to allow cancer cells to multiply in her body more rapidly with such a belief than to hold a more loving and affirming belief about herself? *Our 60-80 trillion cells listen to every word we think and say.* Beliefs like Jamie's, of course, are not the cause of cancer in everyone, for it can be quite different in each of us. One might be more susceptible if continually exposed to toxins, for example. Yet another might be exposed but not get sick since they have few uncleared traumas or negative beliefs. Another might have eaten primarily sugars and simple carbohydrates for years, but even that is an act of not treating ourselves with love. Yet another might have a different belief system, such as: "Everybody in my family gets cancer by the time they are fifty." We must all search for our own answers within, and perhaps we can find what made us more susceptible to effects of sugars or toxins or what made us eat so many sugars in the first place. Two important places to start are to search for uncleared traumas, as discussed in the last chapter, and to identify our uncleared negative beliefs, the two of which work hand in hand.

The ego mind then wanted Jamie to blame herself for making herself sick. Such is the nature of the ego mind. It wants us to follow its directive, like Jamie believing she was rejectable, getting it to be repeated and reinforced, create an illness, and then blame us for having gotten it. It is the classic case of adding insult to injury, which is the nature of the logic of the false self mind. This part of the mind would like us to throw away our power to heal by feeling guilty. But in reality, it is only this illusory mind, our little "i," which wants to blame anyway. Its purpose in getting us to blame ourselves is to keep us from having insight into what we have created and then to keep us from embracing the same internal power to create something positive, such as healing and happiness, instead. Ironically, if we follow the ego mind's lead and feel guilt, then we would cause an even greater disturbance in the mindbody. But let us not throw out the baby with the bath water. Instead, let us simply witness and see through the deceptive and self-destructive logic of the ego mind, thereby disempowering it totally. Dorothy, in *The Wizard of OZ*, found it was as simple as dousing the wicked witch of the West with a bucket of water! Ours might be as simple as doing some bilateral stimulation of the brain or touching some acupressure points while holding a statement of clear positive intention.

Once Jamie had cleared her old negative beliefs (using the EFTA described in the last chapter and demonstrated in the video), she wanted new software to live by, so she decided upon her own wording: "I am a loving person because I am love. I give and attract love and acceptance into my life." She used the Occipital Hold, which I will describe shortly, for installing her new "software."

Tribal Beliefs

The tribe in which we grow up and live determines many of the belief systems we live by and shape what we think of as truth, becoming a part of the operating system for our lives. We might think of our family system as our tribe, or it might be the culture, or a subculture such as a religion or region of which we are a part. Often there is a convergence of the two. Consider the following example of a family tribal belief.

Barbara's family, consisting of her husband and two children, would get debilitating strep throat at least three or four times a year. It would start with one family member and then spread to each of the others one by one. Barbara was a strong believer in the germ theory and the contagion theory, firmly convinced that it was inevitable that once one family member invited in the streptococcus they would all have to contract it or more accurately, make a contract with it. While in our larger tribe we carry such a belief system, Barbara's family manifested this unshakable belief to the nth degree. She believed each one in the family would necessarily catch it from the others, rendering each one a victim whenever the strep was going around.

Consider our tribal mind language: "contract" and "catch." Does it not take some effort to write a contract or to catch anything someone tosses at us? If we do not reach out with intention, whatever is tossed to us will simply fall away. Or we can step aside from something we do not wish to catch. Nor do contracts happen by themselves. Yet, in spite of our colloquial language which suggests some intention on our part, we continue to believe that these things happen to us. We also have a tribal mind belief that "when a bug is going around, we are very likely to catch it." And when we do, instead of looking inside to see why we might have needed to invite it in by reaching out to catch it, we just blame it on the bug that's been going around, or on being exposed to it by someone. Our false self mind wants us to continue to hold such beliefs within our tribe, even though it costs us millions and millions of dollars in lost work days, as well an enormous amount of unnecessary suffering.

I am not saying that germs do not exist, nor am I saying there is no such thing as contagion. But why do some get sick repeatedly while others remain strong? Why do we invite those germs in at one time and not at another? We might reply by saying that my immune system in not as strong at one time versus another. This is true, but even this does not get to the underlying why behind it, for our immune systems cannot be separate from our minds. Yes, we might have been under stress which weakened our immune system. But again, being under stress is not something apart from us out there. Again, it is not a cloud which blew in over our heads. It is mostly our own thoughts about or our interpretation of an external situation or person which bring us varying degrees of stress, even more than the circumstances. We need to attend to our perceptions which cause the stress. The Torah states it so clearly when it says: "We don't see things as they are. We see them as we are."

As long as we continue to keep the tribal mind thinking that stress happens to us, then we will most likely continue to get sick, often frequently, and perhaps even seriously. But we do have another choice: Instead, we might ask ourselves:

What is the source of my stress?

Is there another way of looking at this situation?

Can I interpret it differently?

Can I hold different thoughts about it?

Can I take a healthy action?

Can I make a healthy life style change?

Are their more uncleared traumas fueling my negative beliefs?

Does my inner slave driver or inner judge keep me from living healthily and taking really good care of myself?

How am I not fully loving myself?

Am I able to practice forgiveness of myself and others?

Or, if we can allow ourselves more genuine curiosity without reverting to the ego mind's desire to blame, we could ask, "Why might I need this symptom now?" and the other Six Questions I ask myself. But *we must do it without self blame and guilt.*

Barbara and all the other family members continued to suffer from strep year after year, believing there was no way out of their victimized state of existence. Then they came to believe that the cause of the strep was something in their house, which prompted them to sell it and buy another one across town. But unfortunately, the little streptococci followed them all the way across town to the new house! Their belief system had led them to an expensive move which did not solve the problem.

One day, Barbara told me that her 10-year-old daughter, Wendy, wanted to talk to someone about some concerns she had, and asked if I would be willing to see her for a few sessions. We had made a good connection as we talked for three sessions about her problems. However, as she came in for the fourth session, I could tell she was quite distraught. When I asked her what was upsetting her she said that she was coming down with a sore throat that she had gotten from her father and her brother. She was upset because her annual Girl Scout camping trip was coming up in a few days and that if she got sick she would not be able to go. When I asked her what made her think she would be too sick to go, she replied: "We all always get really sick when we get strep. My father and my brother had a bad case, so I know mine will be, too, like always happens," which was her family belief.

I then asked her if there might be any reason she would not want to go on the camping trip, whereupon she exclaimed: "No way! All my best friends are going, and we always have the best time on these camping trips. I've been looking forward to it for weeks! Damn this strep throat! I wish I didn't have to get it all the time." And she burst into tears. I boldly replied: "You don't have to get sick and miss your trip." I had no idea what her response might be, but her little face perked up from the tears and she excitedly said: "Really? Is that really true?"

I said, "Yes. You have made it clear to me that you are not afraid of going, that it has always been a very enjoyable experience for you; that you always enjoy being with your friends on these trips; that there is no reason you would not want to go."

"That's right!" she exclaimed. "But what can I do? I'm coming down with one of those horrible strep throats like we always get. Once it starts in any of us, it just gets worse and worse!" she declared.

I replied, "Your body has an instant messaging system. It communicates whatever we are thinking and feeling instantly to all the cells in the body. And your body is like a good little soldier. It follows orders promptly. And then I added, "If you really mean it, you can say: 'I really want to go on that camping trip with my friends this weekend, so I am not going to welcome in the strep. I plan to stay totally healthy so I can go and have fun with all my friends!'"

"I'm going to do that right now," she said excitedly and confidently.

I must admit that I felt a little apprehensive about having made such a bold statement. Would she really succeed? Have I set up a situation that would cause her to lose trust in me? I wondered. But I reassured myself that it was not an empty and impulsive statement, but one which came spontaneously both from a deeper intuition which I have learned to trust as well as my personal and clinical experience. Wendy bounded out of the office joyfully, with me saying, "I hope you have a wonderful time with your friends on the camping trip."

I pondered and questioned my statements to her as she left, I thought, "why would I be hesitant to make a positive statement to her which would help her embrace her deep inner power to be healthy and get what she wanted?" Doctors are not hesitant to make pronouncements on the negative side, such as, "it will probably take you a week or two to heal from such and such." I would certainly not want to program in the negative suggestion, which is the thinking within our current tribal mind. Nevertheless, I was not only happy for Wendy, but also somewhat relieved when I learned from her the next week that indeed she had banished her strep throat, and that she had gone on the fun camping trip with her girl scout friends. (As I am typing this story, I caught my tribal mind concept about to come through when I almost typed these words: "and the strep throat went away." If I had written these words I would have been giving the power and volition to the streptococci who decided to go away instead of to Wendy who had the power to banish the strep.) Such is the type of tribal language expression we all need to be vigilant to catch in order to transcend the limiting thinking of our tribal beliefs which so often becomes self fulfilling.

A few weeks later, her mother, Barbara, was getting her first symptoms of strep throat, and said to me for the first time, "I wonder if I could do what Wendy did." Now Wendy had begun to change the tribal belief system in her family that they all had to be contagious and then all had to get sick. It reminded me of the phrase from the Bible: ". . . and a little child shall teach them." Now Barbara was starting to doubt the validity of the family tribal belief for the first time herself as a result of Wendy's success. Once Wendy and Barbara had succeeded, her brother and her father began to change their beliefs as well. Now they all remain healthy with no more strep throats. They had healed the thinking in their minds that thought the body needed to get sick and that they had to catch the strep throat from each other.

Let us look at just a few examples of beliefs in our tribe which can influence us negatively. I'm sure this list will spark a number of others, bringing them into your awareness.

Some Examples of Limiting Tribal Beliefs

**(A printable PDF version of this is on my wcb site:
www.henrygrayson.com for your convenience)**

For any of the tribal beliefs listed below that you think you
might possible hold, place a check:

_____ Money is the root of all evil (instead of <u>love</u> of money
or <u>attachment</u> to money).

_____ I pulled my back because I bent the wrong way.

_____ My genes are doomed.

_____ It's not possible to retain outstanding health.

_____ Sickness comes from something that happens to us.

_____ Marriage will make me happy.

_____ You have to have failing health and go into a nursing
home before you die.

_____ Money and success will bring me happiness.

_____ My upset stomach must have come from something
I ate.

_____ Success comes primarily from what you do, not from
what you believe and think.

_____ Having kids will make me happy and worthwhile.

_____ Memory fades as you get older.

_____ I will most likely catch the cold or other bug that is going around.

_____ Being under stress comes from things that happen to us.

_____ I must have money, success and stuff to be loveable and worthy.

_____ Life has to be a struggle.

_____ Age is such a bummer—everything breaks down.

_____ If we can't see it, it is not real.

_____ Going to the doctor regularly is what will keep me well.

_____ My mother (or father) had diabetes (or another illness), so I'm sure I will get it too.

_____ Miracles can happen only rarely.

_____ I can't be a miracle worker.

_____ I can't heal myself.

The Belief That the Body Operates Apart From the Mind

William Shakespeare's oft quoted phrase: "Nothing is good or ill, but thinking doth make it so," seems to apply to Barbara's family. As they were able to change their beliefs about the inevitability of getting strep throat, beliefs that were just congealed thought systems, they totally changed their minds' need to welcome the strep into their bodies to multiply. *The body does listen to every word we think or say, especially if we truly believe it.* This is true whether or not the belief or faith is in positive or in negative things. It is the same power. If we can dis-cover the power we used to make ourselves dis-eased but without any guilt it is much easier to own the same power to make or keep ourselves well and happy! Otherwise our intrinsic power remains hidden and we preserve our belief in victimization.

It is so easy in the prevalent thinking of the tribe to believe that the body is separate from what goes on in our minds. *Even when we come to accept that there is a mind-body connection, we will still function and think in ways that show that we do not fully accept that there is an inseparable unity—mindbody.* Even the statement, mind-body connection implies that something was separate and we have made a connection. We have not fully understood that there never has been and never can be a separation, and that mind is continually manifested in the body.

How often have we heard two different people with some sneezes and sniffles say quite different things. One will say, "I think I caught it from my co-worker" or "my child brought it home from school. I can tell it is going to one of those doozies." And sure enough it is. Another person will say, "I've been driving myself too hard lately. This is a good warning. I'm going to get to sleep early tonight, and make sure I set aside regular time to do my meditation and yoga each day. When I wake up tomorrow I'm sure I'll be fine especially if I take a few excess things off my plate." And he is! Both are beliefs and instructions being manifested.

Yet another person, upon getting the sniffles, might say, "This is a call to attention. I know I have not taken the time to mourn the loss of my friend who moved away, or the loss of the contract I was so counting on signing which would bring me a huge bonus. I need to take some time to feel my sadness and loss directly." He does, and the cold does not develop. A cold, having the same symptoms as crying, can sometimes mean that we need to deal with a feeling of loss or sadness somewhere in our lives.

When we pull our backs out, we will often say "it is because I bent in the wrong way." We are expressing a belief which will make or keep us sick. It is far better that we realize that we have bent in that way thousands of times before, but why did we pull a muscle this time? There is most likely a reason in our minds for our pain which our illusory minds would prefer we not see, but instead continue to believe the suffering comes from any place else external then the ego mind can have us stay in suffering longer. We must remember that the illusory mind is like the Thanatos, or death wish, which Sigmund Freud observed was present in everyone. But even more, the egoic mind is the part of our minds which wants our misery all the way on the road to death, while promising us pleasure and fulfillment. Yet it always lies, is truly "the wolf in sheep's clothing," "the great deceiver," or the "sly serpent," *and its solution to any problem always creates more of a problem sooner or later,* especially when we retain our limiting negative belief systems. Therefore that part of our minds will always try to get us to see the source of any problem, whether in our bodies, in our relationships, in our finances, or in our success as being outside us completely separated from our minds where we have the power to do something about it. But can't we change the beliefs in our minds far easier and more successfully than we can change the outside world? Duh!! Also, the most effective way to change the outside world is to change our minds first, attending to our negative or limiting beliefs, for mind is all interconnected, there being just one mind in the universe, according to physicist Shroedinger.

Since the idea that our bodies are separate from our minds and that we are separate from others and everything else in the universe is just an illusion, we might even call such a belief a kind of universal hallucination. Since the entire universe is just one unified field of consciousness and energy, there is no way any one of us or any part of us can be separate from this field. Can we expect any organ in the body to function separately from all the other parts or separate from mind? If the field includes everything, then how can any of us step outside it? We are therefore part of The All That Is, which many have called God. As such, we are powerful creators with our thoughts just has religions have seen God as creating with thoughts, such as, "And God said, let there be light."

People will often come around me when they are developing or in the midst of a cold or the flu, they will often say, "I won't get near to you today, because I don't want to give this to you." This reflects their belief system that they could give it to me. I believe it is important to stop the words "give this to you" from sinking into my mind. I do not want to accept that outcome, so instead I say to myself, "I choose to stay healthy. I do not need to welcome in that bacteria or virus today." And I then I add a compassionate thought that the person will return to inner peace. As a result I have never caught a cold from any of my patients, family or friends, over the decades of their exposing me to their germs even when hugging. Whether or not I catch it is up to me, for I would have to reach out with intention to catch something. In that moment I have gotten past the tribal thinking to realize that it does not control me. The "it" does not have the power. But as long as we perceive the outside it as having the power, then it is our reality.

We are the effectors, not at the effect of, our true identity being part of Source energy and intelligence. It is much like St. Paul in one of his letters when speaking of the miraculous things he has either survived or accomplished, he said, "It is not I that does these things, but the Christ who lives in me." What he means by this is the Christ consciousness is the higher intelligence and power of the universe, whether we call it Christ, Yahweh, Spirit, God, Buddha nature, or Higher Self. No one religion owns this Power, for it is universal. Would it not be arrogant and even prideful of us, and would it not create more of the illusion of separation for us to think *I* have the right way, and the other religions are all wrong because they describe this Higher Power a bit differently or use a different word to designate it? Such a position has caused wars and countless deaths, the opposite of spiritual love, therefore is anti-religious, since the root word of religion is religio, meaning to join. It just means that the ego has sometimes invaded our religions, too, since they are made up of other humans with egos.

The tribe of which we are a part has greatly influenced our thoughts, our perceptions, and most of all, numerous central beliefs we live by. If our tribe believes that physical problems are largely caused by external things, and that the only cure can come from something outside, then it will be so for us. If our tribe does not believe in a loving God, but rather in a punishing God who will send us to eternal hell and damnation after we die if we break his laws, then we are likely to carry much guilt and fear. If our tribe believes we have to catch the latest bug going around, then it will be so for us. If we believe the only way to success is through struggle, then we, like Sisyphus, will always be struggling, always pushing the proverbial stone up the hill, but never reach the top of the hill and have a nice peaceful picnic enjoying the view.

Most doctors base their prognoses on the old Newtonian science, and when there is something that happens outside of this paradigm it is explained as a spontaneous remission which is no real explanation at all. When my doctor saw through an X-ray that the severely degenerated disc in my back had regenerated, he exclaimed: "You won't believe this, Henry. This is not possible! It just doesn't happen." I replied, "I do believe it." Such potentialities were not within his world view and its belief system.

Our tribal mind is quite susceptible to suggestions, especially since we believe that most illness comes upon us from an external cause. This is why we will race to a doctor or the drug store in search of a pill to fix it, or why we think we have to catch the latest virus if we don't run to get a flu shot which often does not deal with this year's strains anyway. And now many news reporters and health agencies will encourage people to run out quickly to get a flu shot, which for a significant number of people will actually produce an episode of the flu itself. We will follow the thinking of the tribal mind without any assessment of our own regarding whether we are giving up our inner power and even that we have a choice to embrace it. It's like falling into line behind five or ten other cars at a toll booth when two other lanes are wide open.

Before going any further, *I must reiterate once again that I am not recommending that we abolish contemporary medicine or that we should stop using it.* It has brought us many effective means of healing various bodily symptoms, alleviating much suffering for multitudes of people. We may need to use it regularly until we can see and embrace the power in our minds without being threatened by the magnitude of our inner power. And certainly we will need to use it in emergencies, in certain surgeries, or symptoms we have not been able to heal. Sometimes such a change in our view of ourselves, the power we have, and what is possible in the world would be too threatening to own all at once. In such instances, we should not abandon other forms of alternative or allopathic medicine, but perhaps begin more slowly to change our Newtonian world view to a quantum or spiritual world view where we see infinite potentiality. Then we might proceed in a more gradual way to belief in our Power, which arises along with clearing our barriers to healing and happiness.

Tribal Beliefs About Change

Tribal beliefs affect our attitudes and practices regarding how health and illness take place. Jerome Frank, M.D., when he was a professor at Johns Hopkins Medical School, was one of the major grandfathers of psychotherapy research. He did one study in the 1960's in which he compared three different methods of change: (1) psychotherapy, (2) the Chinese Communist techniques of brain washing, and (3) the religious conversion experience, studying some of the revivalist groups in Appalachia. For example, a man could be a drunkard, beat his wife and kids, be unable to hold a job, and frequently get into bar room brawls making no positive contribution to the community. But, he changed instantly and dramatically, stopped beating his wife and kids, was able to hold a job responsibly, and started making significant contributions to the community. We might wonder, "How could this be? How can such extreme changes take place so quickly? Do such changes last?" The best explanation I can give is that he was part of a tribal mind belief system that believed it to be possible, and also a strong belief that God could and did do it. It reminds me of a statement attributed to Jesus in the Bible when someone was healed: "It is your faith that has made you whole." Being a non-religious Jew, Dr. Frank had no investment in the outcome of the study from a Christian perspective. If anything he was biased toward psychotherapy and science, and was surprised to dis-cover that the religious conversion experience was the most powerful agent of change of the three. It required, however, a joined tribal belief for it to be so powerful.

Most of us live in the midst of a tribal mind belief that change has to be minimal and slow. Having been trained originally as a psychoanalyst, I remember teachers and supervisors telling me that change was a slow and arduous process. Sigmund Freud had said, "The most you can expect from a successful psychoanalysis is to be relieved of some of the worst of your human suffering." Such thinking, as well as some forms of spiritual thought, have become a integral part of a tribal belief system we live by and believe to be true. *The good news is: It is only a belief!* I had an amazing experience which challenged this belief system for me.

When my youngest son was about eight years old, I thought it could be fun for us to build a Japanese type arched bridge over a little stream that ran through the property where we lived at that time. Since he was big enough to drive in nails with a hammer, I thought he would enjoy doing that part of the work with me. After we finished hammering in the nails on the flooring together, it became time to put on the railings. We had soaked 2x4's so that they would bend without breaking. I then began to attach the railing to the posts, using a power screwdriver with very long screws, long enough to hold the railing in until the bend set in on the 2x4's. The screw I was using did not seem to be going into the wood, so I looked down and saw that the head of the screw was stripped. I reached with my fingers to pluck out this damaged screw, not knowing it was extremely hot. When I touched it with my forefinger and thumb, it seared both like a piece of chicken placed in a hot frying pan. Both of us could hear the sound, see smoke from it, and of course I felt the pain. It turned the skin on my fingers white, again like a piece of chicken in a frying pan. The burn was clearly visible to me and to my son.

Normally, I would have stopped work and gone into the house for some kind of first aid treatment of the burn. For some totally unknown reason, I heard a little voice in my head say, "It will be alright." And again, for some unknown reason I totally believed it without any question, and resumed my work. I thought of it again about 15-20 minutes or so later, looked at my fingers, and they were totally healed! Having been burned a number of times in my life, I could hardly believe my eyes, but I could believe that the pain and the skin damage were gone entirely. In my statement, "Oh, it will be alright," I had somehow totally believed it, which is what brought the instant healing.

Somehow, I think the Universe wanted me to get an important lesson that day or perhaps I was just ready to get that lesson—that healing or change can occur at a bodily level as fast as a change of thought in my mind. That experience temporarily took me out of the tribal mind thinking that such a quick healing would be impossible. Even though I had read stories of yogis performing such feats, the Universe needed me to experience it first-hand. I must confess that I have not been able to have the pure enough belief to do it again in the subsequent two or three smaller burns I have experienced, although I did get them to heal much more quickly than in the past. But I did learn that it is possible to heal instantly by doing it once. I just need to fully and completely believe it without an ounce of doubt or attachment.

In the Quantum world, where consciousness intervenes to determine whether energy will slow its vibrations to become matter, it gives a different spin on this experience, as well as those demonstrated by certain Indian yogis, shamans, indigenous healers, and even what doctors call spontaneous remissions, which ignores the role of consciousness in matter. It caused me to think differently about another statement attributed to Jesus in the Bible: "If you have faith so much as a grain of mustard seed, you can say to that mountain, move from here to over there, and it will be so." I used to think of this solely as a metaphor. But with the Quantum world view, I now think that if we could truly know that the mountain is mostly empty space, just dancing energy and information, *and* had a purity of faith, then it could likely be done literally. The brain is just an organ of the larger mind or consciousness. Perhaps our limiting tribal mind thinking keeps us locked in to unnecessary diseases, scarcity, failure, and unhappiness. Just as physicists posit that there may be multiple universes out there, perhaps there may be multiple universes right here that are not visible to us because of our belief system. Perhaps they are existing at a different vibrational level that we can allow ourselves to see. We do not hear sounds that dogs can hear, for example. Yet they do exist.

Any time I hear from someone that they got a diagnosis that the doctor said was incurable, I always feel like questioning: "Is that necessarily true?" I have seen too many people heal themselves of so called incurable prognoses. Sara Beth was diagnosed with stage-four stomach cancer, her stomach protruded out several inches from the tumor. We dove into a crunch program of clearing out a number of traumas she had suffered in her life. More recently, she was disturbed by a very difficult marriage which ended in a highly contentious divorce. We used the EFTA to do a clearing of each of these traumas. Then we proceeded to clear the trauma of moving from her homeland in Poland to the United States as well as not knowing how to speak English and was sent to school unable to communicate with anyone.

Next, we cleared the developmental trauma of growing up with two extremely critical parents. Then we discovered that she had two very entrenched beliefs which most likely related to her sickness: (1) "I don't deserve to get well and be happy since my parents were never happy." and (2) "People will stop loving and showering me with attention if I get well."

Sara Beth also worked to enhance the effectiveness of her chemo therapy by daily instructing the chemo to go directly to the cancer cells, but only to the cancer cells, which significantly decreased the side effects of the therapy. A few weeks later her oncologist declared in amazement, that her cancer markers had dropped from 2, 260 to 179, saying, "This exceeds my wildest expectations." And a few weeks later when they performed surgery to remove the remainder of the tumor, there was none there. The surgeon declared, "It's a miracle!"

Not all people have such outstanding results, however. Charlotte, also diagnosed with stage four stomach cancer, cleared a plethora of traumas and beliefs, first showing great improvement, then taking a dive downward and dying rather quickly. There were two very important beliefs that she had not yet gotten to for clearing, which perhaps could have made a difference: "my cold and rigid family, who are now being caring and taking care of me, will only love me if I am sick," And then "I will not have anything meaningful in my life if I live." Whether clearing these would have made a difference, no one knows. While we can often get to many of the causes of cancer and other sicknesses, sometimes we may not be able to identify all of them in time. But is there anything to lose by searching diligently for the causes which can be identified and cleared?

Doctors twice told me I would need knee surgery in order to heal my torn meniscus from two different ski injuries. They told me surgery was necessary to remove a bone spur in my heel. They told me I would not walk again without back surgery when I had a severely degenerated disc with intense nerve involvement. On the other hand, I was not able to heal a hernia, and had it repaired surgically. Yet I was able to heal all of the others without surgery as well as repeatedly nipping colds and viruses in the bud for decades. But if you are not ready to do self healing, or think your situation is serious enough that you may not have the time to accomplish the healing, by all means, use the traditional medical interventions to stay alive so you can work on self healing in a less life-threatening situation first.

CHECKLIST TO IDENTIFY
NEGATIVE BELIEFS

**(A printable PDF version is provided on my web site:
www.henrygrayson.com for your convenience)**

It can be difficult for many people to identify the negative beliefs that may be contributing to their sickness or unhappiness. Below, I've listed some sample beliefs many people have to help you identify your own. You may find that some of the beliefs that you check off relate to conclusions you drew from the traumas you identified in

Chapter Four. But whether you see a connection or not, you can still identify and then clear your negative beliefs—and then actually install new software which you would prefer to have as your new operating system in their place.

Place a check by all the ones that seem to apply to you in any ways affecting your happiness, health, relationships, or success and rate the strength of the belief from "1-10".

_____ I am worthless

_____ Failing is unacceptable

_____ Yelling will get me attention

_____ I don't have what it takes to do self-healing

_____ I am basically a weak person

_____ No one ever listens to me

_____ I will get the illness my mother or father got

_____ I will die from this illness

_____ I am not loveable

_____ I am undeserving of love

_____ I cannot be assertive without danger

_____ Love will go away

_____ Love will smother me

_____ I will inevitably be rejected

_____ People will betray me

_____ I can't succeed

_____ Success is dangerous

_____ I don't deserve closeness

_____ I cannot be myself for I will be rejected

_____ I am not enough

_____ I must always please in order to have love

_____ Life has to be a struggle

_____ Communication is contentious

_____ Sickness will get me love and attention

_____ Old people will lose their memory

_____ I have to serve everybody else

_____ I'll probably catch the bug going around

_____ The doctor will fix my symptoms for me

_____ My body is frail

_____ I have always had a weak system

_____ My boss doesn't like me

_____ It's better not to try rather than try and fail

_____ I'm destined to be a victim

_____ I'm too old to _____

_____ God will punish me

_____ I will deteriorate with old age

_____ Fighting is a way to connect emotionally

_____ I don't deserve success

_____ I will be controlled or overpowered by others

_____ I must do what everyone else wants me to do

_____ I must struggle in order to succeed

_____ Sickness happens to you

_____ I will be rejected if I initiate sex

_____ Marriage will make me happy

_____ Abundant success is unsafe

_____ I don't have much to give

_____ To argue is to connect

_____ If I get close, I will lose myself

_____ If I can't do it perfectly, than I'd better not do it

_____ Closeness is dangerous

_____ Everyone knows more than I do

_____ I'm not attractive enough

_____ I'm not worthy of success

_____ I don't deserve perfect health

_____ It's not safe to be perfectly healthy

_____ My work cannot be fun

_____ I'm not worthy of a happy and healthy life

_____ I'm controlled by my genes

_____ Sickness will get me out of things I don't want to do

_____ I can't find enjoyable and fulfilling work

_____ Sickness is a way to show my vulnerability

_____ I can't succeed more than my parents

_____ Life is burdensome

_____ I catch colds and flus easily

_____ I will be abandoned

_____ I'll hurt someone if I get angry

_____ I will be rejected

_____ I am unlucky in life

_____ I am unattractive

_____ I just can't seem to make it

_____ Everyone has to get sick

_____ I always have to work like a slave

_____ Money will make me happy

_____ I don't have the power to keep myself healthy

_____ Germs make me sick

If you have any of these or similar beliefs, you are likely to make them self fulfilling prophesies, or you will do your best trying. See if any of these beliefs feel familiar to you. See if this list can spark your thinking about other tribal beliefs you might have. You might begin to make a list of limiting beliefs your family had, or the people around you have. Which of these do you think you might be living out in your life?

ADDITIONAL NEGATIVE BELIEFS YOU HAVE IDENTIFIED:

IF YOU HAVE DIFFICULTY IDENTIFYING YOUR NEGATIVE BELIEFS, look at the list of common complaints below. If you often feel one or more of these experiences, place a check beside them:

_____ rejected	_____ worried	_____ ignored
_____ not listened to	_____ self involved	_____ deprived
_____ lonely	_____ controlled	_____ powerless
_____ depressed	_____ afraid	_____ not respected
_____ weak	_____ tired	_____ selfish
_____ unloving	_____ a failure	_____ sick
_____ critical	_____ inadequate	_____ agitated
_____ incapable	_____ controlling	_____ nervous
_____ too giving	_____ tense	_____ powerless
_____ afraid of sex	_____ not listened to	_____ a failure
_____ unable to sleep	_____ withholding	_____ unfairly treated
_____ desperate for sex	_____ afraid of affection	_____ aches and pains
_____ not good enough		

AFTER HAVING ONE OF THESE EXPERIENCES ASK YOURSELF:

Is there something else I might have concluded about myself, other people, family, relationships, health or sickness, marriage, work, or the world as a result of

the above experiences? Write them here or after the feeling words you checked:

_____

_____

_____

_____

LET US NOW USE AGAIN THE <u>EFTA</u> PRESENTED IN THE LAST CHAPTER ON TRAUMAS, AND USE THAT PROCESS FOR CLEARING EACH OF YOUR NEGATIVE BELIEFS. AGAIN, YOU MAY FOLLOW THE EFTA IN THE VIDEO WHICH YOU CAN VIEW by visiting my web site <u>www.henrygrayson.com</u>, or use the instructions that follow. Note that the "set up" is slightly different for clearing negative beliefs than it was for clearing traumas.

EFTA

An Adaptation of the Emotional Freedom Techniques (EFT) by Henry Grayson, Ph.D.

1. Breathe slowly and deeply into the diaphragm while placing your finger on the lower forehead, above and between the eyebrows. Focus on the negative belief, or the negative identity you wish to release while continuing to breathe slowly and deeply.

2. Allow scenes, images, or memories which represent the negative belief to come into the forefront of your mind. It might be one scene

or a series of scenes. Allow scenes which could have inspired such a belief to begin with—as well as those that reinforced it as time went on.

3. Notice what emotions the scenes or memories make you feel. Identify the emotion(s).

4. Notice where you feel the emotion(s) in your body and focus your attention there.

5. Then, move your finger onto the inside edge of the eyebrow and say: "I now release all fear related to this belief." Breathe slowly and deeply.

6. Next, place your fingers on the outside edge of the eye and say: "I now release all anger, resentment and rage related to this belief." Breathe slowly and deeply.

7. Place fingers on the bone under the eye and say: "I now release all anxiety related to this belief." Take a slow and deep breath.

8. Place fingers under the nose and say, "I now release all embarrassment related to this belief." Breathe slowly and deeply.

9. Place fingers under the bottom lip (at the indent) and say, "I now release all guilt and

shame related to this belief." Take a slow deep breath.

10. Place fingers under the arm, about 4 inches down from the armpit, and say, "I now release all excessive concern related to this belief." Take a slow deep breath.

11. Place fingers of both hands under the rib cage on both sides and say, "I now release all hurt and sadness related to this belief." Breathe slowly and deeply.

12. Place fingers on chest cavity about 2-3 inches above bottom of rib cage and take several slow deep breaths as you inhale love into your heart and exhale fear through your solar plexus.

13. Place fingers on and below the collarbone (about where a button down collar would be) and take a slow deep breath.

Check your level of disturbance of the belief on the "0-10" point scale. If it is not down to a zero, repeat until you bring it down to a zero.

Let us start to question any limiting belief that we carry or which surrounds us in our tribe's belief systems. *If you have to doubt anything, first doubt your limitations.* Doubt your negative beliefs! To doubt such beliefs will take us to times of confusion and further doubt. We will doubt old beliefs and we will doubt our potentialities. But if we do not have doubt and confusion, we are probably still attached to expecting the worst thinking about what is possible or not possible. I am told that in Bali there are gargoyles guarding the doors to their temples: one is named Doubt and the other Confusion. The symbolic meaning of this is that we must go through doubt and confusion to reach insight or enlightenment. We often need to go through doubt to let go of an old belief which our tribe has lived by. Confusion comes when we are letting in a new possibility to mix with an old or limiting concept that is cherished. It may be that our biggest doubts are indeed creating our most stubborn limitations.

Installing New "Software" And Opening New Neural Pathways

When we have lived by an old belief system for a long time, it is most familiar to us. When we have an old program installed in our computers, it takes up space and will only print out what the old program allows. The old software of our negative belief systems not only needs to be deleted, but we also need to install new software.

As we saw, when we were very young, we downloaded much software from the people about us, who mostly were not qualified to know how to write an operating system for their lives. And then we used these downloads, models, and streams of information to write our operating system for our lives when we had no idea about how to do it. Yet we did the best we could. We now have a chance, not only to get rid of our undesired old software, but also to install new software which we would prefer to live by now.

All the neural pathways to support the flow of that information have been opened wide, making the old thought and belief patterns most easy to fall back into. It is much like a wide and deep channel that has been eroded away in a big creek bed. In order to get the water to flow in a different direction we must open up a new channel.

Not opening new neural pathways is why so many people easily fall back into their old thought patterns, negative beliefs and behaviors even after they have cleared their traumas and negative beliefs. Many people do not get the success they desire from just reciting positive affirmations or holding positive images, not only because they have not cleared out their traumas and negative beliefs, but also because they have not opened up the new neural pathways.

The <u>steps</u> we need to take in countering this problem are:

1. First, clear the old traumas
2. Next, clear the negative beliefs which grew out of the traumas
3. Then install new "software," which is replacing the old negative belief with a positive one you would now prefer to live by and have as your automatic operating system.
4. And finally, do the exercise below to open new neural pathways to support the new positive beliefs thereby making it easier to begin and sustain new positive thoughts and behaviors.

Now that you have cleared your traumas and negative beliefs, it is time to take Step 3 and install a new positive belief as your new software.

Installing the New Software

1. Select an old negative belief which you have cleared.

2. Think about what statement would express the opposite of what you have cleared, one which you would prefer to have as your new operating system. Make sure that the words say it exactly the way you want. For example, if you previously believed "I do not deserve abundant health and happiness," one might choose for the new belief: "I totally deserve abundant health and happiness." If it has been, "I will always be rejected," you might consider, "People like me and are very attracted to being with me." *Make sure there are no double negatives!* The right brain will just get the image, and not get the "not" or "no longer" statements, and you could be reinforcing the wrong thing!

   Often the new positive statement will not feel like it is true at first. Your ego mind will often shout out, "That's not true. You can't say that. You would be lying." The ego mind wants you to repeat the negative past, not wanting you to engage in an act of new creation that brings joy and health. Remember the definition of faith: "Faith is the *substance* of things hoped for . . ." We are now beginning the opening of new neural pathways by experiencing in our minds the substance of what we are now inviting into our lives.

The Occipital Hold For Installing a Positive Belief

Assess the strength of your belief in the positive statement on a scale of 0-10. (Use self assessment or do muscle testing). Sometimes it will have come up a few points just because you effectively cleared the negative belief. The goal, of course, is to bring the strength of the positive belief up to a "10".

1. **Place one hand across the forehead leaving your eyes exposed, and place the other hand on the base of the skull in the back of the head (covering the occipital lobe).**

2. **Close your eyes, if you are comfortable doing so, and take several slow deep breaths. Inhale with your tongue behind your front upper teeth and exhale through slightly pursed lips in order to help slow down your brain waves from Beta to Alpha.**

3. **Begin to repeat the positive statement you have decided upon as your new belief, saying it to yourself meaningfully. You might emphasize different words each time . . . Say it with authority . . . . If you have said the negative statement to yourself with intensity, make the positive statement with at least equal intensity.**

4. Make up an image which represents the positive statement . . . . Let it become clear and three dimensional . . .

5. Notice what emotion you feel when making the statement and holding the image.

6. Notice where you feel the emotion or emotions in your body and focus there.

7. Hold all four together: the positive statement, the image which represents it, the emotion which arises from them, and where you feel the emotion in your body, and state firmly to yourself (preferably aloud): "I NOW KNOW ALL THIS TO BE TRUE! AND I KNOW IT TO THE VERY CORE OF MY BEING."

8. While continuing to hold the pose, take several more slow and deep breaths while you make the positive statement to yourself, with authority, holding the image, feeling the emotion, and focusing on where you feel it in your body, while you keep the Occipital Hold, <u>open your eyes and look to the left, and then to the right, to the left, and then to the right</u> (continue back and forth about 15-20 times).

Release the pose. TEST THE STRENGTH OF THE NEW BELIEF AND <u>REPEAT THE PROCESS UNTIL YOU REACH A "10"</u>, meaning that you totally believe the new statement. You can find a download of this process on my web site, www.henrygrayson.com which you can use for your installations.

OPENING NEW NEURAL PATHWAYS

When you have cleared your traumas, cleared your negative beliefs which grew out of them, and have installed the new software of your new belief, you still need to open up new neural pathways. The new messages from your brain need to become habit. The old research we used to read about habit formation concluded that we needed to do a new behavior for about a month or for about 70-74 times. What we did not know until the advent of neuropsychology and brain scan studies is that new habits are simply the opening of new neural pathways.

Simply repeat the above Occipital Hold Process about two times a day for about four weeks. This will help you open up the new neural pathways enough to become habit. Why does this process work?

(1) When you hold the frontal lobes of the brain with one hand and the occipital lobe at the back of your brain with the other hand, you are sending strong subtle energies through the entire brain and stimulating one of the pleasure centers in the brain.

(2) When you breathe in through the nose with the tongue behind the front upper teeth, you are slowing your brainwaves from beta brain waves to alpha. This means that your brain is prepared to be more responsive to the suggestion you are about to make, as though you were in a light hypnotic trance, making

it significantly more effective than if you did not use this form of breathing.

(3) When you make the positive statement to yourself strongly and with repetition, you are stimulating the left hemisphere of your brain.

(4) When you make up the image which represents your new positive belief, you are stimulating the right hemisphere of the brain.

(5) When you identify the emotion which the statement and the image evoke, you then anchor it in your body by focusing there.

(6) When you make the declaration aloud and with intensity, you are reinforcing your commitment to the statement.

(7) When you open your eyes and move your eyes back and forth, left and right, while holding the statement, image and feelings together, you are activating the left and right hemispheres of the brain and the front and back of the brain to work together on assimilating this information.

So you can see that this simple process can have some powerful effects on your brain to help you open up new neural pathways to make your new positive belief a habit. The ego mind will try to get you to forget to do it, or it might say, "it takes too much time!" The fact is, it only takes 2-3 minutes a couple of times a day which can have a positive effect on your whole life working better and even more efficiently.

Remember, the ego or false self mind will want you to forget to do it so you can stay in pain or suffering longer. *To get it going, and especially to keep it going, it is best if you schedule it into your life right along with some other regular ritual which is already in place,* such as before brushing your teeth, immediately after rising, just before going to bed, or when you first arrive in your office, then it will be easier to remember and do it so you can begin to reap the benefits.

DOWNLOADS

When we are little children, we absorb everything around us like little sponges. We don't even think about it. Our brain waves are so slow it is like we in the equivalent of a deep hypnotic trance. In the first year or two of life, we are in delta brain waves and in the remainder of the pre-school years, we are in theta brain waves—the two slowest brain waves we humans have. And then throughout grammar school we are in alpha brain waves, which is like a light hypnotic trance state.

When we want to plant a suggesting in someone's mind, we may use hypnosis to help a person get into slower brain waves, for then they are much more susceptible to taking it in more deeply. For example, if we want to help a person stop their smoking habit, we might plant the suggestion that they hate the taste of cigarettes. The slower brain waves help them take in the material more effectively. This is why a young child at three years of age can easily learn three languages at the same time, if they are spoken around her. But the same child would have to work very hard to learn these same languages at a teenager!

We download many very useful things, such as language, walking on two feet instead of all fours, and a multitude of things to help us function well in the world. On the other hand, we may download mom or dad's pattern of dealing with conflicts, how they handled stress, how they communicated, how they dealt with challenges, and a multitude of other things. We may also download their beliefs about health, sickness and healing. We may download their patterns of dealing with illnesses or staying healthy. We may download their fears, guilts, pressures, and demands. We many download their attitudes about being powerless or having some kind of control in the world. We do all this as if our brain computer was connected to the internet to receive any sort of download–but we did not have to type in any command, it just happened.

Once we have gotten clear about what we downloaded from our parents which we do not want to keep, we can use the EFTA for clearing these downloads. Only the Set Up for the procedure is a little different:

Set Up for Clearing Downloads With the EFTA

1. **Assess the strength of the specific download you wish to clear on a scale of 0-10.**

2. **Place your fingers on the center of the forehead as in clearing traumas or negative beliefs.**

Begin to focus on the behavior or attitude you downloaded from your parent which you would like to be free of. Notice what you feel as you remember scenes of that behavior or attitude . . . . Then, focus on any scenes which denote you playing out that behavior or attitude in your life. Notice what each of these scenes make you feel, and where you feel the feelings in your body.

Then, with the intention to clear the download, follow the EFTA process described above for clearing beliefs or traumas.

Continue to repeat the clearing process with the EFTA until you are clear that the strength of the download is a "0."

CHAPTER 7

There Are No Idle Thoughts

You are what you think.
With your thoughts you make your world.
Gautama, the Buddha

In spite of such ancient wisdom, and more recently the advent of cognitive therapy, it is quite difficult for most of us to absorb the fact that *there is no such thing as an idle thought*. Every thought we think has an effect on our moods, on our bodies, our relationships, our successes and failures. For most of us, it seems as if our thoughts are running us. We may not be "put in jail for what you're thinking," as in Rogers and Hammerstein's *South Pacific*, but these thoughts can surely put us into a hellish mindbody prison.

Our thoughts can potentially affect the more than 50 trillion cells in our bodies up to 100 times more powerfully than a physical or chemical environment. This means that literally it is our thoughts that can make us sick even more than a bacteria or a virus and perhaps even more than some cancer cells which we may have in our blood streams at all times. Is it our thoughts which make a significant difference as to whether they multiply and grow? Much evidence points to that conclusion. *Our thoughts can make us heal or stay sick* but our tribal mind thinking is so accustomed to seeing ourselves as victims in this world, meaning we see the source of illness as outside us and the cure as outside us. We see the source of unhappiness as outside us and the solution as outside us: "if only the circumstance or person will change, then I will be happy." All the above causes us to disown our intrinsic internal Power and perceive ourselves as essentially victims.

To review a basic premise: Our thoughts make the cells in our bodies happy and peaceful, or they make them jittery or depressed. Our thoughts cause our internal complex chemical factory to produce oxytocin and make us peaceful, or they produce the stress hormones cortisol and adrenaline in response to our fears and pressures. As we have seen, our stress is not so much related to the external event, but how we interpret the event. It is not what the other person did or did not do, as much as our thoughts about what they did or did not do that determines whether we are stressed or at peace. Even how, when or which genes are activated is directly related to perception, according to the new science of epigenetics, meaning that which is above the genes. Our genes are activated or deactivated by environment, but the environment includes what we think, perceive, and interpret. It is not the genes which rule, as we were taught in school, for now we know it takes the proteins to activate the DNA. And the proteins are dependent on their receptors for information in the environment. The environment's most powerful communicator is energy and what we think is expressed as a mode of energy.

We saw earlier that the *New England Journal of Medicine* reported that at least 80% of physical symptoms presented to primary care physicians are stress related, and we saw that stress is caused by our interpretations and thoughts, it is clear that our thoughts are intrinsically involved in sickness or health. This means that only about 20% of the time our symptoms are from other causes. And then we learn that only 5% of people have illnesses which are genetically caused, which means that most of us have incredible power of choice as to what we do in our minds and life styles to affect our cells. Therefore, we need to fully absorb the following reality:

If I focus on worry thoughts, I make my mindbody weaker.

If I focus on angry thoughts, I make my mindbody weaker.

If I focus on resentful and vengeful thoughts, I make my mindbody weaker.

If I focus on how I have been victimized, I make my mindbody weaker.

If I focus on anxious thoughts, I make my mindbody weaker.
If I focus on negative judging thoughts, I make my mindbody weaker.

If I focus on hopeless thoughts, I make my mindbody weaker.

If I focus on rejection thoughts, I make my mindbody weaker.

If I focus on fearful thoughts, I make my mindbody weaker.

If I focus on helpless thoughts, I make my mindbody weaker.

If I focus on thoughts of hatred, I make my mindbody weaker.

If I focus on how I want to get back at someone, I make my mindbody weaker.

If I hold thoughts of littleness, I make my mindbody weaker.

If I focus on how burdened I am, I make my mindbody weaker.

If I focus on how unfairly treated I am, I make my mindbody weaker.

If I focus on how I have been or will be abandoned, I make my mindbody weaker.

If I focus on how deprived I am, I make my mindbody weaker.

And if I focus on some of the above thoughts, I'm also much more likely to have an accident. The accumulation of the various kinds of negative thoughts continue to make our immune systems weaker and weaker over time. How can they not but produce a physical, emotional (i.e., anxiety or depression) or relational symptom sooner or later? Sometimes they will be minor and sometimes quite serious.

"How does this work?" one might ask. <u>TO REVIEW</u>: every time we rehearse any of the above thoughts in our minds, we begin to feel it as if it is happening now. When that occurs, the limbic system becomes activated to help us survive the danger. Even though the danger is not actually present in this moment, when we are thinking about the danger, our bodies react as if it were now, secreting the stress hormones adrenaline and cortisol, depleting the serotonin level in the body, making us depressed. Also, when the brain goes into survival mode, the rest of the body reacts as well. First, blood flow is constricted to the logical and problem-solving part of the brain, the frontal lobes, while the blood rushes into the limbic system to help with survival. When the blood flows away from the frontal lobes, we actually become less intelligent and cannot solve problems as thoughtfully or creatively. But the brain is not the only part of the body affected. Since we need to survive, blood goes into the arms and legs in order to aid us in fight or flight. But unfortunately, it takes the blood away from the digestive system, which is necessary in order to process nutrients for the immune system. When there is not just an immediate danger, such as narrowly avoiding stepping in front of a truck, but we rehearse dangers of the past or future in our minds, the body experiences it as happening now. This system for survival worked fine for the cave man when he had to run to the cave to escape a tiger or a charging buffalo, for as soon as he was safe in the cave, the threat was over, and the limbic system could return to rest and homeostasis. But when the repeated stressful nows go on and on and on with our thoughts, it is understandable that our immune systems become depleted, gradually making it more likely we will get sick. Rebbi Nachman of Breslow, the wise Hasidic master in the late 1700's, put the truth so simply but profoundly:

You are where your thoughts are.
So be sure that where your thoughts are is where you want to be.

Banish Guilt

As we recognize that our thoughts can make us sick, *we must be sure that we do not blame ourselves or feel guilty about having such thoughts.* Blame and guilt would be just another layer of egoic-mind thinking to keep us in suffering and help us become even sicker; guilt is also a frequent factor in creating illnesses. *A Course in Miracles* boldly states that "guilt is always insane and has no meaning." The egoic mind, our false self, would like us to be distracted by the guilt so we will not monitor our thoughts. Then we can suffer longer and be more prone to get sick. Instead, let us rejoice when we become conscious of negative thoughts in our minds, knowing that when conscious, we can just observe them and then choose to let them go. In doing so, we are taking back our power and taking ourselves out of a victimized or powerless perspective.

Guilt, in the ego logic of the world, demands punishment. So, if you feel guilty, then your thoughts are used to punish yourself. And one way you do that is by attacking your immune system and other cells, bringing an illness sooner or later. Our guilty thoughts are much like having an enemy within our gates working as a subversive agent to destroy our power. Yet, we are the ones in charge of what we think. As Pogo expressed it in the old comic strip, "We have found the enemy and it is us."

The Nature of Thoughts

Social psychologists have found in various research studies that we have a huge number of thoughts each day, possibly at least 30,000. Some studies suggest it could be as many as 70,000. That fills a lot of the 1,440 minutes we have each day. A careful analysis of these thoughts will reveal that a huge majority of them are often quite negative and as many as 90-95% of them are often repeated day after day. *All these thoughts are producing effects,* especially when we entertain them by inviting them in to visit for a while, sometimes as a live-in house guest.

Our minds race about from one thought to another endlessly. Some people have referred to this phenomenon as the monkey mind, because our thoughts act like a group of monkeys leaping from limb to limb, screeching as they go. Others describe thoughts like a herd of wild horses stampeding out of control. In either description, our thoughts seem to create an existential hell in mind and body. John Milton, in his classic work *Paradise Lost,* stated it aptly: "The mind is a powerful place. It doth make a hell of heaven and a heaven of hell." This thought cycle rehearses the trauma, the negative beliefs, and any of the barriers that emerge from the trauma and beliefs. Thoughts about past traumas, as well as thoughts that echo negative beliefs, reinforce their supposed truthfulness.

You may ask, "Can I really change my thoughts? Isn't this way of thinking just who I am, resulting from my genetic makeup and my childhood experiences? Aren't these patterns fixed, and I should just accept this as being who I am?"

The 300-year-old physics and linear world view of Isaac Newton would say yes, as if we are hopelessly determined by our past. But contemporary research in infant and child development concludes that all of us throughout our childhoods and into adulthood are constantly interpreting and re-interpreting ourselves through our interaction with our environment, our relationships, our experiences, and our interpretations of them. Indeed, how a child interprets his or her experiences is also a major factor in personality development. What this means is that our interpretation, even as little children, is part of the environment which can override genes and other parts of the physical environment! If we changed them once, we can change them again. In fact, change is the only thing constant in the physical universe. While these thoughts may seem so relentless and powerful, the truth is that they have no power at all except that which we give to them by listening to them, believing them, and then rehearsing them.

Further, in a Quantum world as portrayed by the New Physics, a world where the invisible realm, including consciousness, is far more powerful and mysterious than the visible one we know. Here, thoughts have profound effects and even transcend time and space. We saw that Astronaut Edgar Mitchel was able to send telepathic messages from outer space to a person on earth, with accuracy that was highly statistically significant, and that thoughts affect the outcome of random number generators, as multitudes of trials revealed from the PEAR institute research at Princeton. We saw that physicist William Tiller, retired chairman of the Department of Material Sciences at Stamford University, has developed an apparatus which can record how consciousness and thoughts actually affect physical space.

A few decades ago I was fortunate to hear Cleve Baxter speak at a "New Dimensions in Consciousness" conference in New York City telling about a very unusual discovery he had made from an impromptu experiment in his laboratory one night back in the 1960's. Baxter, America's foremost expert in the polygraph (lie detector test), was working in his laboratory late one night and decided to boil some water to make himself a cup of instant coffee. While waiting for the water to come to a boil, he noticed his dracaena plant, a tropical plant with large leaves like a palm tree. He wondered, what would happen if he wired the polygraph to this plant? Would it react to stress the way humans do? Thereupon he decided to wire the polygraph and see what would happen. After wondering what could create anxiety in the plant, he decided that burning a leaf could probably do it. Borrowing some matches from his secretary's drawer, he walked to the plant, took out a match, and at the *intention to strike the match to burn the leaf, the polygraph* sounded off dramatically! Puzzled by this, he thought that he must not have wired the plant correctly. After checking all the wirings, he proceeded once again with his impromptu experiment. Once again, *at the intention to strike the match to burn the leaf* the polygraph reacted. After several more attempts the next day to replicate this experiment, he continually got the same results. However, when he just pretended he was going to burn the leaf, the plant did not react.

His conclusion was startling to him: He did not have to actually burn the leaf to get a reaction. He only had to have the intention! If he did not actually intend to burn the leaf, the plant knew the difference! The plant actually responded to his thoughts of intention! This and many other carefully carried out experiments using the polygraph to show how thoughts effect plants were later reported in the fascinating book, *The Secret Life of Plants.* We are gradually seeing how our thoughts affect anything and everything around us, so our bodies cannot escape the profound effects. Baxter's impromptu experiment was highly consistent with what I had learned from Physicist David Bohm: "There's no sharp distinction between thought, emotions, and matter. The entire ground of existence is enfolded in space."

An easy demonstration with muscle testing shows how our thoughts either strengthen or weaken a person. In this example I have found that if I ask a person to extend his arm and resist my pushing it down while thinking a negative thought, we found that the arm went weak and if they were thinking a joyous or loving thought, the arm became strong. Now, if I give a secret signal to one person (John) who is to think the positive or negative thought, but then test not only his arm, but also the arm of another nearby person (Gregory), then Gregory's arm becomes strong or weak according to the John's thoughts even though Gregory had no idea which thought John was thinking. Such a demonstration infuses stronger meaning to the oft quoted phrase from Mohandas Ghandi: "We must be the change we wish to see in the world." If I can change my own thoughts, I change not only my own inner world, but also my body world and then I also change what I perceive as the outer world.

"When we are healed, we are not healed alone," states *A Course in Miracles*. Our own healing always reaches outward to unknown numbers of people about us. Therefore, we should never feel selfish about our healing, for as we heal ourselves, particularly the healing of our minds, we are also healing others. But, when we withhold healing from ourselves, we are withholding it from others as well. Such is our interconnectedness, breaking through the illusions of separateness.

If we have any remaining doubt about how our thoughts affect our bodies, consider the work of Japanese scientist Masuru Emoto. Professor Emoto would take distilled water and place words on the glass or test tube overnight, such as "Love and thanks" versus "You make me sick. I will kill you." Then he would freeze the water and take pictures of the water crystals, which are as follows: If our bodies are 68% water, imagine how each thought is affecting our cells with our positive or negative thoughts. Is it any wonder that our thoughts can make us sick?

Water Crystals with the words, "Love and Gratitude"

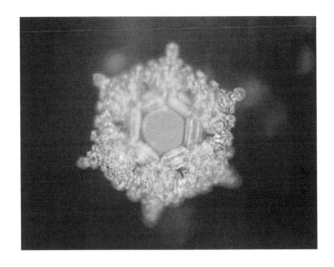

Water Crystals with the words, "You Make Me Sick, I Will Kill You"

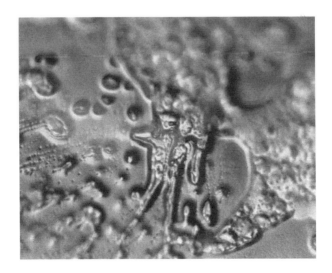

Consider some of the common thoughts we have which can profoundly influence our bodies' responses. Take time to read this list slowly, pondering each one to see if it is familiar to you as one of your thoughts:

My job is killing me.
I'll catch this cold (flu, etc.) from you.
I need a break.
I don't want to go to _____.
I don't want to do _____.
I don't care if I die.
I need rest, but I can't take the time.
I need to be taken care of.
I'm tired of struggling.
I always get the flu each winter.
My allergies are bothering me.
I just want the doctor to fix it.
I need a way to get out of _____.
I just want to die.
I am so exhausted.
I am so stressed and I can't take it any more.
I know I am coming down with _____.
I must always struggle.
I am a bad person.
I must pay for my guilt.
I am a failure.
I am not loveable.
I will always be abandoned.
My back is killing me.
_____ person is driving me crazy.
Additional thoughts you may have:

—————————————————————————

—————————————————————————

—————————————————————————

—————————————————————————

Next, let yourself imagine for a moment what your body might do in response to listening to each of the above thoughts. As you reflected on the list, you might have become aware of additional negative thoughts which you tend to focus on. Make a list of them, think of how your body might respond to them, and then <u>choose</u> whether you would like to have that emerge as an actual result in your life.

You might think of each of these thoughts, and others like them, as programming that your body will respond to positively or negatively. Be careful when you think these thoughts, for your body will listen to you. Remember, it is basically like a good little soldier; it follows orders and suggestions as well.

As we saw earlier, we draw conclusions from our painful childhood developmental experiences (traumas), which congeal into basic negative core beliefs which we described in the last chapter, and these work much like the software in a computer program. Until the encoded information to do with the emotional charge on these traumas or beliefs has been cleared, both the traumas and the beliefs will continue to attract or create repetitions of these negative and painful experiences, even though we strongly disliked them. It is these uncleared traumas and the software of negative beliefs that we concluded from them (core beliefs) that gives impetus to the repetitious thought patterns we think over and over throughout each day.

Even if we clear the effects of traumas and the negative beliefs, if we do not change our thought patterns, we can reactivate the traumas or re-establish the software of our negative beliefs.

But as I have described, these clearings can now take place rather quickly using one of the tools (see Appendix for Quick Reference of all Tools described in the book), or you can contact a practitioner through the resource guide at the end of the book to assist you.

If you are wondering how the effects of our early experiences (the traumas and negative beliefs) can be cleared, when we experience them as having such powerful effects in our lives, you must remember that our world is also a digital world. This is how your computer works. There are no words, pictures, music or colors in your computer just a series of incredibly fast ons and offs. Since the computer contains only encodings of information, and our brain is the prototype of the computer, then our brains and our mindbodies contain encodings of information. We learned how we can use one of the methods described earlier to delete the emotional charge on the earlier trauma or to change the negative belief, much like deleting an unwanted program in your computer, thereby making it easier to monitor our relentless negative thoughts. Please do not forget for a moment that these thoughts are not innocuous, but are always affecting the health of our fifty to eighty trillion cells! *Remember, there is no such thing as an idle thought.*

Our thoughts are not so much observations as they are powerful acts of creation. Notice what feeling follows inside of you with each I AM statement. Sit with each thought for a moment and notice the effect:

I AM tired.
I AM happy.
I AM energetic.
I AM lonely.
I AM deprived.
I AM whole and complete.
I AM no good at _____.
I AM very good at _____.
I AM successful.
I AM sick.
I AM a failure.
I AM loveable.
I AM not attractive.
I AM worn out.
I AM old.
I AM health itself!

You might continue by making up an infinite number of such statements and notice the difference in the way you feel after each positive or negative statement. As you declare I AM, powerful forces of energy converge to support the statement. Notice how your energy and joy go down when you make the negative statements, and how more upbeat you feel with the positive ones. You will also notice that the egoic mind (the false self) may want to argue with you over the positive ones. If so, it is often likely that the negative side of that statement is a belief that needs to be cleared.

Our most repetitive thought patterns will most often be rehearsing our most cherished beliefs, positive and negative.

By becoming aware of our thought themes we can also begin to identify more of our core beliefs are which are affecting our lives and bodies adversely today. The negative beliefs will need to be cleared, of course, with one of the exercises described in the last chapter and demonstrated in the video, in order to sustain our health.

Our thoughts trigger many of our emotional responses. If we have thoughts of sadness, we will feel sad. If we have thoughts of happiness or love, we will feel happy. If we think thoughts of scarcity, we will feel deprived. If we think thoughts of gratitude, we will feel fulfilled. If we think thoughts of pain, the pain is likely to increase. If we think we will get sick, it is more likely that we will. Even a diagnosis or a prognosis can have devastating effects. Our thoughts and emotional responses always trigger reactions in our bodies (as you will see quite clearly in Chapter Eight).

Thomas, for example, suffered from debilitating irritable bowel syndrome, which was especially difficult for him since he was a traveling salesman. But gradually he began to let himself become aware of the connection between his thoughts and what happened in his body. He conveyed his excitement over his discovery one day to me as he said, "Henry, I've discovered that if I allow anxious thoughts to linger in my mind more than 30 seconds, I have to run like crazy to a bathroom and I have trouble making it! If I catch them in less time my stomach remains at peace." Thomas used his awareness to take back his power, instead of projecting the power onto his bowels as doing something to him.

If you think you will have trouble getting a good night's sleep, it will likely be true. If you allow disturbing thoughts to linger in your mind, you can also find your sleep disturbed. If you think you will be fully rested in the morning, you probably will be. If you think you cannot take time off to rejuvenate, you probably won't. If you think you can work it out, you will likely find a way. If you think a task will be difficult, it will be more so. If you think you can learn it quickly, you will be more likely to do so. Henry Ford recognized this in his often quoted saying, "If you think you can, or you think you can't, you are right."

There is a poignant phrase from *A Course in Miracles* which I have repeated to myself for years as a reminder about the role and power of my thoughts: "It is my thoughts alone which cause my pain." And then I typically add another one which gives me the redemption from my negative thoughts: "I can elect to change any thought that hurts me."

These statements have been enormously helpful to me to cease projecting the cause as external in another person or situation, and then to take back my power over my thoughts, my mind, and my body.

Mindfulness and Meditation Can Help

Meditation is a way of becoming more aware of the thoughts which run through our minds endlessly, and to begin to take back control of what we think and where we focus. It is actually a form of mind training. Meditation is essentially picking something to use as a focal point in your consciousness, and repeatedly choosing to focus on it. The focal point could be a word, a phrase, a tone such as ohm, a flicker of the flame on a candle, a positive phrase, the breath going in and out, a chant, or even a repeating prayer. One easy meditation is to imagine you are breathing love into your heart and that you are exhaling fear out down through your solar plexus.

You do not have to focus perfectly to be successful. What is important is that you actually sit and keep coming back to your focal point. Your mind will drift off to a multitude of different things, but you keep coming back to focus. It is much like training a horse to follow the most gentle tug of a rein. When he starts to move in a different direction, the trainer gently, ever so gently, gives a little tug on the lead, keeping the horse on course in walking around him in the ring. We do the same with our thoughts. We are not harsh or even judging of ourselves. Certainly, we are not to call ourselves failures if we do not stay focused. We just gently come back to focus again and again. Our success lies in continuing to practice our imperfect meditations. You will find a guided meditation in the video download to help you get started.

If you fly from New York to Los Angeles you will be off course about 90-95% of the trip, yet you still arrive at your destination. Even though the air currents may continue to blow the plane off course, the pilot steers it back on course repeatedly, which is exactly what we need to do with our thoughts. We must give up the expectation that we have to do it perfectly. Instead, let us just continue to become aware when our thoughts have drifted off and bring them back to focus. It is a meditation practice. We practice what we want to get better at. So let us just keep practicing, again and again, reaping the benefits of doing so, knowing we will do it quite imperfectly.

As we learn to bring ourselves back to focus on our predetermined point (word, breath, tone, etc.), we become aware of the different thoughts that go through our minds.

We can just simply observe them, and gently return to our focal point. We are then training our minds to go where we want our thoughts to go. The tail does not so much wag the dog anymore.

While some people can use various mindfulness techniques or thought-monitoring exercises to take charge of which thoughts are allowed to stay in their minds, others feel overwhelmed by the over abundance of relentless negative and disturbing thoughts which run through their minds. Some people have given up their attempts to meditate because they experience their thoughts as being like a stampede of elephants, totally out of control, and they feel powerless to take back control. Quite often, this block is due to the fact that the traumas and beliefs which inspired such thoughts have not been cleared. It's like several diesel engines pushing a train powerfully at the same time we are trying to apply the brakes. Such an experience of fighting against ourselves can leave us exhausted! It is no wonder we might develop such symptoms as depression, chronic fatigue, fibromyalgia, and other autoimmune diseases where the body appears to be attacking itself. It can be helpful to think of the autoimmune attacks as a manifestation of us attacking ourselves in our minds and behaviors, now just expressed in bodily form. Our highest conscious self does not want to attack ourselves, but the judging and often vicious egoic thoughts we allow to linger in our minds are doing a momentous job of self attack, spilling into the immune system.

Judy, for example, had persistent, fearful thoughts that men would leave her. These thoughts would start as soon as she began to let a man become important to her after dating a handful of times. She would dwell on those thoughts endlessly, imagining how he would become interested in another woman, or how he would be transferred by his company to another city, or worrying that he would die from his high-pressure job. There was no peace in her mind. It was only after clearing out the traumas of her parents divorcing, resulting in her father moving across the country and rarely ever seeing her again, and her mother now working long hours away from home, and then spending a lot of time with her new boyfriend, that she could begin to be successful in monitoring her thoughts of abandonment. Further, the clearings of these traumas and the belief that she would inevitably be abandoned, enabled her to do the thought monitoring and to sustain the practice of meditation as a form of mind training. All were necessary for her to regain her health, since she had been suffering from bouts of fibromyalgia. A further belief was that "only if I am sick will mother stay home and care for me," which was about the only time her mother was available to be nurturing to her. This belief continued into adult life, and she therefore continued to believe that would happen with anyone who became family or important to her. While this belief system was intact, to give up her physical symptoms would be risking never getting love!

After these traumas and beliefs were cleared, she could successfully monitor her thoughts about abandonment, thereby allowing her body to begin to heal and her energy come back. It was not the necessary passport to love any more. Therefore it allowed her to sustain a successful ongoing and loving relationship with a man for the first time without living in constant dread of abandonment, which would destroy the relationship by getting him in some way to abandon her.

Another Important Reason for Thought Monitoring

It is also important to remember that when we clear out our traumas, they are cleared. But if we keep thinking about that trauma and reliving it, we can reactivate that encoded information. Similarly, we can clear out a negative core belief; however, if we keep dwelling on thoughts which might rehearse that belief, we actually begin to rebuild it. If you demolish a brick building, but each day you stack up some of the bricks again on top of each other, you begin to reconstruct the building. Therefore, after we clear our traumas and core beliefs which are driving the negative thoughts, it is imperative to monitor our thoughts or we can reactivate or rebuild those influences. We need to work on it from both ends. *Just as it is often necessary to clear out our traumas and negative core beliefs in order to be able to monitor our relentless negative thoughts, it is also necessary to monitor our negative thoughts in order not to rebuild the negative belief or to rehearse or reactivate the original traumas.* It is necessary that we continue do our personal work at all levels to retain our happiness and health, regardless of whether we take a medication or have a surgical procedure, or even take natural herbs or have acupuncture. But before your egoic mind has a chance to get you to think of thought monitoring as too much work and therefore too tiring, think of how much more you will feel burdened, get sick, and remain in suffering if you don't do it. In this spirit, I think of it more as play than work.

We desperately need to identify our negative thought patterns and not let them continue automatically. Otherwise we throw away our power to keep healthy, happy, and successful. We had the highest rate of combat neurosis from our war in Vietnam, more than any other war in our history. Why? The soldiers quite often did not know who the enemy was. Danger did not lie only in a North Vietnamese soldier in uniform, or a jeep with their emblem on it. It could be a child, a mother with baby in arms, or even a grandfather who would reach inside their clothing and toss a hand grenade into the soldier's jeep. Sometimes the soldiers would mow down innocent people who were reaching a hand inside their coats, not out of hostility, but out of their fear of being killed the very next moment if they didn't preempt the hand grenade attack. Then they would be overwhelmed with guilt over having killed unarmed and innocent civilians. Not knowing who the enemy was literally drove many soldiers batty.

It is much like that for us. When we do not identify which thoughts that are our enemy thoughts which cause us pain, suffering, weakness, unhappiness, sleeplessness, anxiety, worry, depression and much physical sickness, our entire mindbodies are driven batty. Until we recognize the thoughts which cause us harm and learn ways of letting them go, we will continue to suffer needlessly.

Just as it is difficult for us to build a house or repair a car without tools, I believe we need many tools for our psychological and spiritual growth. We need tools to help us create health. We also need tools to take charge of our thoughts, such as the ones below.

Tools for Becoming Conscious of Your Thought Patterns

One easy place to start is by committing yourself to making a written or mental note of the thoughts you have just in the first hour after you get up. People are often amazed at the prevalence of negative thoughts just during that first hour of the day when they are setting the tone for the rest of the day. Many have exclaimed, "I had no idea so many of my thoughts were so negative!" Their thoughts have become so routinely automatic and the bad feelings which come out of them are so familiar that they seem perfectly normal. But then they wonder why they feel sooo bad, sooo exhausted, and attract sooo much negativity into their lives, their bodies and their moods.

Step One: Becoming More Conscious

The following exercise is one many people find extremely helpful in increasing their conscious awareness of the thoughts in their minds. It is quite simple, but people report profound results:

1. Carry around an index card and a little stub of a pencil for a couple of days.

2. Every time you become aware that the thought you are thinking is negative, or become aware that the thought you just had is taking away your peace, say:

There is one of those enemy thoughts, just here to make me suffer.

This does not mean that there is an actual enemy out there somewhere, but rather that the thought system in our minds is an enemy type of message and not a voice of truth or friendship.

3. Take two or three slow deep breaths as you simply place a check on the card.

Why does this work? First, you are being mindful of your thoughts, consciously identifying any thought that disturbs the peace in your mindbody, which is any negative thought. By saying "There is" you are dis-identifying yourself with the negative thought. Secondly, you are putting an enemy uniform on the thought, so you do not confuse it with a friendly thought or ally. If you do not confuse this negative thought with the voice of truth, it no longer has any effect on you, for it has no power at all except that which we give to it by listening to it and believing it. It affects you adversely only if you believe it, continually listen to it, and keep reciting its message to yourself. Thirdly, by taking some deep breaths and placing a check on your card, you are breaking into the automatic thinking cycle which would have already spun out several more negative thoughts. By placing the check on the card you are anchoring in your awareness of the thought designated as a negative one which you have identified.

Many people report a great reduction in their negative thought patterns just from doing this exercise for a few days.

Taking Charge of What You Think

This exercise takes you to another level of dealing with that negative chatter in your minds, literally putting you into the driver's seat. The tail is no longer wagging the dog, for the dog can now wag the tail. You are now aware that you have the power, not the thoughts which run through your mind. It is now your choice as to which thoughts you want to invite in for a cup of tea, as an overnight guest, or as an ongoing house guest. It's not that you will stop the thoughts from appearing in your mind, for the egoic mind is relentless and persistent. But now, you recognize that you have the power to decide whether to allow the thought to stay for a visit. One Indian master teacher, Yogananda, stated beautifully his decision about his thoughts when he said, "I never allow any thought to linger in my mind without my express permission!"

The following exercise will help you to regain that power. You will note that the first two steps are similar to the above exercise, but then it builds on them.

The Powerful 18 Second Thought Monitoring Exercise

1. Whenever you become aware that you are not totally at peace, ask yourself:
   What was I just thinking?

   Just asking yourself this question is a very important step. You are no longer blaming some one of some thing outside yourself for your loss of peace. By asking "what was I just thinking?" you have begun to recognize that it is your thoughts about the person or situation that is disturbing your peace. You might not be able to change the person on circumstance, but you can take back the power to change your thoughts about them. Since so much of our disturbance comes from giving up our power to some external person or situation, it is of utmost importance that we begin to take it back and embrace it.

2. As in the above exercise, say:

There is one of those disturbing egoic thoughts. It is here <u>only</u> to disturb me.

Here you have labeled it, placed an enemy uniform on the thoughts so that they are not mistaken for the voice of truth. You have become an observing witness to the thoughts, not identified with them. Most importantly, you have seen this negative thought system for what it is and declared its motive to yourself. In doing this, self deception becomes more difficult. Remember the philosopher Nietzsche's words: "The person we lie to most is ourselves." And the main way we continually deceive ourselves is by listening to and believing the egoic chatter of those repetitious negative thoughts in our minds.

3. Here you move to the place where you will be motivated most strongly to change your thinking. This step is in two parts:

A) Remind yourself of this truism:

Whatever I focus on will surely increase as my reality, both internal and external.

B) Then say to yourself:
"Do I want this thing I am focusing on now to increase as my reality internally or externally?"

When I ask myself these questions, I am more motivated to change. For example:
If I am worried, "Do I want this thing I am worrying about to increase?" or
"Do I want this judgment to increase in my life?" or
"Do I want what I am fearing to increase?"

When I ask myself these questions, I usually answer with a resounding, "NO WAY I WANT THAT!" I also know if I allow those thought to linger, I could be setting myself up for a symptom sooner or later!

The egoic mind will often retort in many of us, saying: "But it is true!" It wants us to keep thinking the thought because it might be a statement of fact at this moment. However, that is not the point. In this exercise, the issue is not about what is factual! The most important point is: *If I focus on it, it will surely increase. If I keep thinking those thoughts I will help to bring more of it about. Do I want that to happen? NO!* Because you now realize that your thoughts are always creating an outcome especially in your body. At this point, you are more likely to be strongly motivated to proceed to the next step.

4. Use an action word to give an executive order which portrays you, the observing You, as truly in charge. It is not a battle with your negative thoughts, for that would only empower them. It is just a realization that if you focus on the thought it will increase, that you are motivated to simply discard the thought. Pick your power word: I . . .

>   *cancel* . . .
>   *dismiss* . . .
>   *delete* . . .
>   *banish* . . .
>   *stop* . . .
>   *exorcise* . . . . *that thought.*

You may also be able to use humor to laugh at the ridiculous logic the ego mind has used. Now that you see it, can laugh at it, you can also totally disempower it. You have ceased seeing this illusion as real.

5. *Then fill in the empty space left by dismissing that thought with an affirmation.* It can be a psychological or spiritual statement, but one which you believe or want to come to believe. Aristotle pointed out many centuries ago that "nature abhors a vacuum," which means that where there is empty space, something will rush into it.

Water will fill a hole first. Air rushes into a low pressure area, creating wind. We now need to fill that empty space in our minds with something positive before the negative chatter comes back in to fill it.

It might be simply reversing the negative thought to something positive. Or, if you cannot quickly think of something, it is always good to have a standard affirmation which you can rely on instantly. Some people have used such thoughts as:

I AM a loving person.
I AM a good hearted and caring person.
I AM likeable at my core being.
God is love, and so am I.
I am happy and healthy.

Others have chosen to have a pre-determined song they would sing or a chant they would use to fill the space. The most important thing is to come up with a phrase which you like. Maybe you already believe it, or you may just want to come to believe it. Either is OK.

The egoic part of your mind may already be saying: "I can't do this. I have so many negative thoughts that I would be doing this exercise all day long!" This is just the ploy of the egoic mind to get you not to do it, and then stay in suffering from your negative thoughts. The truth is that if you do this process, *TAKING ONLY ABOUT 15-20 SECONDS* each time, *you will free up immense energy, increase your focusing and efficiency, and increase your overall health, success, and happiness*. You may have to repeat it a number of times through the day, but the 15-20 seconds it takes could well free up minutes, hours, and days of more productive, happy, and healthy times.

A Simple Tool: The Thymus/Heart Rub

You can also use the Thymus/Heart Rub described earlier to stop negative thoughts. A simple and effective way to break into cascading negative thoughts is to take a deep breath or two and begin to do the Thymus/Heart Rub (pacing your hand flatly on the upper chest, rubbing gently in a circle) while saying aloud, "I deeply love and accept myself, even though I was thinking _____." Or "I deeply love and accept myself, even if I started to let my mind go to negative thoughts." Many find that taking the physical action of rubbing the chest while saying the loving words is a very powerful way of letting go of disturbing thoughts.

Make the statement five to ten times as you do the Rub. Here you are healing the negative thinking with love and acceptance. This method of healing is far more effective than mentally fighting against a negative thought or condemning yourself for having negative thoughts.

Any time you become aware of negative thinking or thought patterns, remember: **My thoughts have brought me dis-ease. My thoughts can bring me ease and health. Changing my thoughts can change every aspect of my life, including my health. In essence, using the above exercise to become aware of ego thoughts and to lct them go is not to be viewed as a big job and hard work. Rather, let us view them as an opportunity to become free—to get out of being a prisoner to the ego mind and the suffering it brings. If we forget to use these tools to change our thinking, it is because we have valued something else.**

CHAPTER 8

Emotions in Sickness
and in Health

*The fact that the mind rules the body is in spite
of its neglect by biology and medicine, the most
fundamental fact which we know about the
process of life*
Franz Alexander, M.D.

Doesn't it seem so much of the time that our feelings
are running us rather than our having chosen them?
Consider these statements: The storm made me so afraid.
He abandoned me and made me terribly sad. They made
me feel so guilty, or I'm so anxious because my boss puts so
much pressure on me! Or it might be: I'm so angry because
she is always judging me! I'm so afraid of making a mistake
and looking foolish, or I could be happy if he wouldn't treat
me that way; he is so critical.

It is so natural for the illusory mind to have us see
ourselves as powerless in the face of what is happening or
what another may have done, that we think our feelings
are happening to us, rather than seeing that our emotions
result from our interpretation and perception of what is
happening. Even the hardwiring of our limbic system, which
has encoding of past pains and traumas, seems to rule us
because that part of our brain literally hijacks the rational

brain. But it is only because so much of the source of our behaviors and emotions are unconscious. But as we have seen, these encodings of information from our past traumas can now be identified and cleared. And also, we can re-train the brain to give different signals to produce different brain chemicals so that they evoke different emotions in our bodies. Consider the following dramatic example.

Remember the numbers of Tibetan monks who were imprisoned by the Chinese Communists and tortured except when they were put away into solitary confinement. After their release, some were brought to New York Hospital to be examined by psychiatrists for signs of posttraumatic stress disorder. Much to the examiners' surprise, they were not able to find any signs of PTSD! How many of us could even imagine not being stressed by such mal treatment? Yet, if it is possible for them, is it not also possible for us? If even one person can do it, it means it is possible. Perhaps we have just not learned how much power we have to choose which feelings we have, just as we have not acknowledged our power to choose what thoughts we think. How often might we say: "But I just feel that way," as if it is the feeling that has the power. Such is the world of duality into which we have come, where we experience and are trained in so many ways to think we are powerless. And it is those emotions we think of as negative which come out of the illusion of separateness, and therefore feel fearful and powerless. These are also the ones which are more likely to contribute to our mindbody sicknesses, whether expressed emotionally or physically.

I have used the tools presented in this book consistently and found them to be helpful to me in embracing more and more of my internal power much more of the time than ever before. As I have done so, I feel a hundred times more in charge of which feelings I had allowed myself to rehearse, and have gotten sick less and less. Can there be a connection? Each time we embrace the power of our minds we are beginning to embrace our interconnectedness with the All That Is, taking back our True Self identity.

William Ernest Henly challenged our powerless view of ourselves in the last century when he said:

It matters not how strait the gate,
how charged with punishment the soul,
I am the master of my fate;
I am the captain of my soul.

MindBody Power over Emotions

Most scientists exploring the mindbody activities conclude that real, physical expressions carry out or mediate these mindbody connections, for there can be no purely emotional or physical illness since they are inseparable. They believe that no thought, no feeling, and no mental change ever occurs without something physical changing in the body. Emotions drive our physiology, for the mind and the brain determine the chemistry, which produce the emotions that are then sent to the body's cells. Literally, our thoughts and emotions can make us sick and keep us from healing; and our thoughts and emotions can make us joyous and healthy! Such a connection was recognized much earlier by Sir William Osler (1849-1919), the father of modern medicine, when he said, "The cure of tuberculosis depends more on what the patient has in his head than what he has in his chest." Unfortunately much of modern medical treatment has forgotten this, even though mounds of research have come forth in recent decades in psychoneuroimmunology and other areas of alternative and mindbody medicine.

Mindfulness teacher Thich Nhat Hanh expressed our choices simply when he said: "Sometimes your joy is the source of your smile, but sometimes your smile can be the source of your joy." It is our choice to miserable or happy and it is most often our choice to be sick or well. We just don't realize much of the time the choice we have. We often do not realize that it is our interpretive perception of the circumstances, our rehearsed thoughts about them, or uncleared traumas which cause our emotions.

How Our Emotions Seem to Make and Keep Us Sick

For decades we have had research that points to cigarettes, fatty foods, life style and obesity as causes of heart diseases and other illnesses. Then, other research began to look at what is behind the surface observable issues, particularly our emotions, which have an even more powerful effect. Hundreds of research studies abound showing us the connection between various emotions and sickness: anger, fear, anxiety, guilt . . . and the list goes on. Anxiety disorders cost the US an estimated $75 billion a year in medical and work-related costs, half of which is spent on treating physical symptoms resulting from the stress of anxiety. As countless studies show, anxiety, as well as anger, weaken the immune system and increase one's susceptibility to illness.

John M. Kennedy, MD, medical director of preventive cardiology at Marina Del Rey Hospital in California, has reported a study done at the University of Southern

California. Seven hundred and thirty-five patients were followed for over 12 years, and the researchers found that anxiety and chronic stress were better predictors of heart attacks than just the previously considered risk factors, such as weight, smoking, exercise, and so on. Their conclusion was that those who reduce their stress responses were 50-60% less likely to have a heart attack than those who continued to experience ongoing or increasing stress without reducing it. But most often, we do not help people learn how to decrease their stress responses by guiding them to go upstream to the source of the stress and clearing out the antecedents.

Similar findings to those above have come from follow-up studies after 9/11 terrorist attacks. Those who experienced themselves as powerless in the face of the attack were more severely traumatized than those who felt they could do something, such as helping others out of the buildings, since fight or flight is a stronger energy than powerlessness. Also, those who continued to be severely stressed (meaning that the trauma had not been cleared) were 53% more likely to have heart problems. They were also twice as likely to develop high blood pressure. Dr. Kennedy explains it thus:

> Chronic stress . . . increases the activity of *platelets*, cell-like structures in blood that clump together and trigger most heart attacks. It increases levels of cortisol, adrenaline and other stress hormones that promote arterial inflammation.

It is important to remind ourselves repeatedly that stress is not just some amorphous thing hovering over us. Nor is it something inflicted upon us. It is based on individual perceptions, interpretations, degrees of unresolved traumas, and amount of learned skills for dealing with life for each of these determine the motions we feel.

VICIOUS INTERACTION CYCLE OF THE EGO

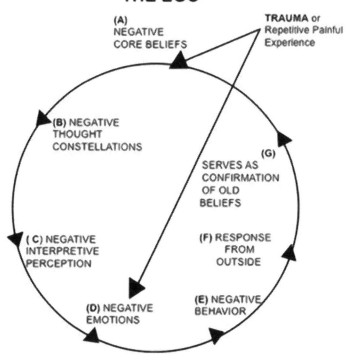

From this diagram, we see that our traumas start out the negative direction of the ego mind, creating the negative beliefs, the negative thoughts, the negative interpretive perceptions, all of which help to determine the emotion we feel.

All these lead to our behaviors, which includes our bodily reactions. Then we also see the line from trauma to emotions, showing how a current trauma or a current trigger can reactivate an uncleared trauma or emotion directly and immediately. When the survival brain, the limbic system, interprets something occurring in the present as a source of danger based on past hurts or dangers, which could be simply a seemingly innocuous occurrence, it immediately arouses strong emotion as designated by the arrow across from traumas to emotion, literally hijacking all rational brain function.

This cycle will continue to go on ad infinitum unless we break into it. And the most effective ways are (1) clearing traumas, (2) erasing negative beliefs, (3) changing our thought patterns, and (4) making a shift in our interpretive perception. Trying to change our behaviors or emotions without these clearings is extremely difficult, most people relapsing.

Emotions are experienced viscerally and throughout the entire human body. Neurotransmitters and neuropeptides found in the organs, spinal fluid, the brain, and in cells all fluctuate in a complex and ever-changing balance to regulate energy, emotions, and health. This is why most researchers in psychoneuroimmunology believe that all *thoughts, all feelings, and all mental changes (including learning) are always accompanied by a physical change in the body, especially in the brain,* whether a one-time traumatic event or the ongoing insidious source of emotional distress or suffering. This is why long-term stress from anxiety, fear, anger, worry, resentments, pressure, guilt, and other negative emotions gradually weakens the brain, sometimes shrinking parts of it, downgrading the nervous system, and particular organs over the course of time. These things do not suddenly pop up as a serious illness. Instead, they have often been germinating for a significant period of time, sometimes short and sometimes long, with stress hormones continuing to flow. But it is very difficult to change our emotion and it is far more productive to change one or more of the four causes of the emotion.

Cynthia, growing up in a suburban town in the midwest, had been abused physically by her mother, who not only beat her, and sometimes dragged her across the room pulling her by her hair, and would also bang her head into the wall or sink. If that wasn't enough, her father would sexually abuse Cynthia and her sister. Her mother would pick her up hours late from school or playtime in the park, and would also lock her outside in the cold as punishment. And on top of it all, both parents would verbally abuse her.

As a result, Cynthia lived in a constant fear, not feeling that she was safe. She never knew when her mother would turn from being nice and playful to suddenly abusive. Cynthia never knew when she might be forgotten or abandoned, creating panic out of the continual uncertainty. Feelings of powerlessness and hopelessness were continually prevalent.

Is it any wonder that she developed a life-threatening illness when she was in her early twenties? Her deeper healing could only begin after she cleared out her childhood traumas and the emotions that accompanied them.

Cynthia's experience reminds us of how when we are feeling one of the derivations of fear and anger, our survival brain kicks in and becomes more active for fight, flight, or sometimes shutting down. When this occurs it takes blood flow away from the digestive system and sends it to the arms and legs in order for fight or flight to occur. When this happens we do not digest our food properly, and our immune system weakens from being deprived of nutrients. If the disturbance is extremely intense, the immune system may weaken quickly. If these threats and their corresponding disturbing emotions are ongoing, the depletion of the immune system is cumulative, sooner or later showing the eruption of an emotional and/or bodily symptom as in Cynthia's case.

But these stresses are not necessary, for we can learn to clear ones that have already happened and often therefore prevent or diminish the level of disturbance of those being reactivated in the future. Further, we can retrain the brain. But our ego minds will inevitably oppose these positive actions. As Pope John Paul II observed insightfully: "The strangest and most fantastic fact about negative emotions is that people actually worship them." Since negative emotions are like Velcro to painful experiences and like Teflon to positive ones, it is no wonder we need so many tools to get past worshipping them and so we can detach from painful emotions.

Impact of Stress on the Body

Let us look at several studies showing what happens when the ego mind has us keep these stressful emotions active.

Margaret Chesney, M.D. at the University of California Medical School has concluded from her studies that anger physically affects the heart itself. In fact, according to a study reported in the *Archives of Internal Medicine*, (Apr. 2002) in a sample of more than a thousand subjects, it was found that young men who quickly react to stress with anger had three times the normal risk of premature heart disease and five times the normal risk of an early heart attack by middle age even with no family history of heart ailments. Edward Suarez, Ph.D. in *Brain, Behavior and Immunity* (Vol. 16, No. 6) found that anger did not have to be full blown to cause bodily trouble. People who carried the attitude of ill-will or resentment toward others in addition to the tendency toward physical harm or verbal aggression have a stronger tumor necrosis factor, a protein that is released by immune cells and other tissues causing inflammation of the arteries, leading to atherosclerosis. No wonder forgiveness is so important to our health!

Stress resulting from fear and anxiety can slow down the healing of wounds, as much as a 40% increase in recovery time, as discovered by Phillip Marucha, DMD, Ph.D. at Ohio State University. Interleuken, a substance integral to wound healing, declined as much as 68% just over the stressful fear and anxiety of students taking exams. What if students routinely used the EFTA to do rounds of clearing their negative beliefs, fears, and anxieties at exam time? Or what if schools offered meditation classes to groups of students? How much might their health and performance increase?

Our inner disturbances, especially ongoing ones, do not stop in affecting just our moods and our bodies. They also affect those about us, for we not only influence our hearts, blood cells, and other bodily systems with our emotions, but also those closest around us, as John Cacioppo, director of the Center for Cognitive and Social Neuro-science at the University of Chicago concluded. His conclusion, therefore, supports the concept in the new physics of the non-local mind and the fact that we are all interconnected in one universal mind. For example, Linda Gallo, Ph.D., reporting in *Psychosomatic Medicine* in 1999, found that either being an angry or hostile spouse, or living with one, put both at a higher risk of cardiovascular problems. On the positive side, a study done at Yale by Dr. Shu-Ming Wang, a professor of pediatric anesthesiology, found that treating acupuncture points on mothers' ears goes beyond the benefit to them, but also has a calming effect on their children about to undergo surgery, and that lowering their fear prior to surgery had a major impact on the ultimate outcome of the child's operation.

Anger not only affects the cardiovascular system, but seems to contribute to depression as well, which in turn weakens the immune system. Strangely, aggressive anger and depression have a similar origin—feelings of powerlessness. What is anger but a defense against feelings of powerlessness and fear? Even schools of acting teach that anger is not a front-line emotion, but rather a secondary emotion, meaning it takes a more vulnerable feeling such as fear or hurt to activate it. Physiologically, the threat response in the limbic system, the survival brain, causes us to secrete cortisol and other stress hormones, which depletes the serotonin balance in the brain, causing depression.

A Howard University study reported in the August 2011 edition of *The Journal of the American Heart Association* found that women with a history of depression had a 29 percent greater risk of stroke. And those who took antidepressants had an even higher rate of stroke; 39 percent. Perhaps it is even more important that we get to what is behind the 80,000 women with depression rather than just trying to change the serotonin balance.

Over all, the extensive studies in psychoneuroimmunology strongly indicate that virtually every sickness that can befall the body, from the common cold to cancer and heart disease, can be influenced positively or negatively by a person's mental and emotional state.

All of the tools introduced so far will help you clear negative emotions (Thymus/Heart Rub, EFTA, and TFT). Just focus on the negative emotion you wish to remove while doing the thymus/heart rub or while tapping on and holding your fingers on the acupressure points. Also, here are two additional quick tools that you can use to let go of negative emotions, before proceeding to the positive-generating emotional tools described next.

EFT Quickie

This is a simple exercise that asks you to focus on a specific negative emotion you are feeling, and then tap 15-20 times on each of the designated acupressure points on the picture below.

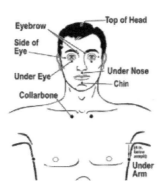

Identify the disturbing emotion (or thought), then as you tap, use intention to release the disturbing emotion.

Tap on the eyebrow
Tap on the outside edge of the eye
Tap on the bone under the eye
Tap on the upper lip, below the nose
Tap under the bottom lip
Tap on the collar bone
Tap under the arm (about 4 inches down from the arm pit)
Tap on the center and top of the head

Breathing from the Diaphragm

Another effective tool that can target and help release negative emotions is the following deep-breathing exercise. Most of us tend to hold our breath or breathe shallowly, which either constricts emotion from our awareness or funnels it into the cells of our body. Others, when taking a deep breath do so when the lungs are half full, but by allowing your lungs to fully empty, you expel all the old carbon dioxide and make room for plenty of fresh oxygen, which helps you both feel and manage your emotions more effectively.

Oxygen is fuel for the brain. Without it, you cannot think clearly, problem-solve fully, or manage stress adequately. Therefore without sufficient deep breathing, you are more prone to anxiety and depression and sometimes sleep problems. On the other hand, when you make a conscious effort to breathe slowly and regularly, exhaling fully, you calm your nervous system and decrease the release of stress hormones, and stop the emotion from running you.

DIAPHRAGMATIC BREATHING:

1. Sit comfortably or lie on your back.
2. Place your hand on your diaphragm, just below the rib cage.
3. Just begin to observe your breath. Is it fast or slow? Is it shallow or deep? Observe it for a couple of minutes. You may notice that your breath becomes slower and deeper as you are observing it.
4. Make sure you are exhaling completely. Push out all the stale air, and hold it for a bit until your body wants to take in the new oxygen. Take it in slowly, deeply, and fully into the diaphragm—not into the chest. Make sure that you exhale fully and hold that for a moment. You might even press your hand on your diaphragm in order to exhale completely.
5. Begin to count slowly as you breathe. You might inhale to a slow count of 3, 4, or 5. And you may exhale to the same number of counts—or perhaps higher numbers for exhaling, such as 5, 6, or 7 or even more.

Such breathing will begin to retrain your limbic system to relax and cease the flow of stress hormones. You will find it easier to quiet the negative thoughts in your mind as well as your breath.

Using these tools and the others offered earlier in the book (clearing traumas, negative beliefs, and negative thoughts) can help you reprogram the way your mindbody reacts to disturbing emotions. You will find yourself lovingly releasing the emotion without suppressing it. You feel it, acknowledge it, and with loving acceptance, you let it go so that the negative emotions no longer disturb your mindbody.

Clearing Downloads

Since we download so many things from our parents and other significant people around us, we can download their way of dealing with emotions: being rageful, stuffing emotions down, being harshly negative or critical, being frightened of many things, or frequently anxious or worrying. We can also download their ways of dealing with conflict, with challenges, or with their sickness and health. You can use the EFTA to clear out any of these downloads where you find yourself repeating your parents' unproductive ways of dealing with various emotions.

Love as Healing Power

Love, portrayed through the centuries as the embodiment of God, is the highest Power. We are part of this power, not *apart* from it. This is not the sky god being portrayed as judging, punishing, and vindictive, which is just a projection of the human ego. Being aware of our permanent connection to Love instantly increases a sense of strength in the body. For example, if you test the strength of a person's arm when they are thinking a thought about fear, worry, anger, or other negative emotions, pressing down firmly on his or her arm when focusing of those emotions, the arm becomes very weak even when feeling anger! Such an experience is very disconcerting to some men who have worked out with weights many hours a week and are very strong. Yet, when thinking about a time they were angry their arms often become so weak I can push them down with one finger even though they are resisting as much as they can. On the other hand, when someone thinks about a time he or she felt compassionate love toward someone, even people who don't work out, their arms become incredibly strong, so strong I cannot push it down trying as hard as I can with both hands! Just our remembering such thoughts can have the same effect on the body as the actual experience.

Fear, depression and anger, all come from feelings of littleness, although expressed in apparently opposite ways. Love is the opposite of fear and anger, and is the higher energy, giving more power. When we realize we are connected to the Source, love makes us stronger and thereby less prone to the opposite emotions which destroy our mindbodies as well as our spirit. Hostility bumps up your blood pressure while nurturing love lowers it. Anger can prompt a heart attack; love makes your heart stronger. We must note however, that if our love is to live up to a religious image, or if it is given in the hope of expectations of something back, then it will do the opposite. It will actually weaken us.

One of many valuable experiments done by the Heartmath Institute in California was one in which some human placenta DNA, the most pristine form of DNA, was placed in a container from which they could measure changes in the DNA. A vial was given to each of twenty-eight subjects who had been trained to generate and feel different emotions. The amazing discovery was that the DNA changed its shape according to the feelings of the subjects. For example, when the subjects felt gratitude, love and appreciation, the DNA responded by relaxing. The strands unwound and the length of the DNA increased. When the subjects felt anger, fear, frustration, or stress, the DNA responded by tightening up. It also became shorter and switched off many of the DNA codes. They then found that these codes could be switched on again when the subjects began to feel the feelings of love, gratitude, joy, and appreciation.

They also found that feelings of love, care, appreciation, and compassion produce a smoothly coherent heart rhythm, as well as absorbing less cholesterol, thereby preventing arteries from clogging. On the other hand, they found that feelings of fear, frustration, and anger cause one to have a jagged, incoherent heart rhythm.

People who are feeling love and joy actually produce more DHEA, the hormone that counters aging and gives us youthful vitality. On the other hand, the stress produced by the negative emotions of fear, frustration and anger produced high levels of cortisol which is associated with Alzheimer's, depression, diabetes, and numerous other illnesses as well.

In a later follow-up study, the HeartMath Institute did a testing of patients who were HIV positive, and found that when the patients had feelings of love, gratitude and joy they created 300,000 times the resistance in their immune response than they had without those feelings!

I knew of one man, the uncle of one of my former students, who had leukemia. When he learned of the Thymus/Heart Rub, known to boost T-Cells, he said he began to do it many times a day as he walked around his house, saying as he rubbed his chest saying: "I deeply love and accept myself even though I have leukemia. I deeply love and accept myself, even though I'm feeling scared. I deeply love and accept myself even though . . . ." and he would fill in the blank with whatever negative emotion he was experiencing. He reported that his T-cell count increased significantly each time he went to his oncologist while doing this exercise.

In communication, the Heartmath Institute also has revealed, the heart energy is 60-100 times more powerful than the brain. So if we bring our thoughts down into the heart, thinking with love and compassion, we actually put a rocket booster on our thoughts. Consider what this must also do to our cells, and also what it sends to those around us.

Consider another intervention which produces no harm. Far better than taking a medication with harmful side effects for your high cholesterol, how about trying what one study with healthy college students revealed. In this study, students were assigned to two groups: Group one wrote about their loving affection for a meaningful person in their life; Group two simply wrote about other topics. All participants wrote for 20 minutes on three separate occasions over a five-week period. Total cholesterol was measured at the beginning and end of the study. The results: Cholesterol dropped by an average of more than 10 points for those expressing love in their writing, while there was no change in cholesterol at all for those writing on general, non-love-focused topics.

There are at least 500 studies demonstrating that unselfish love is extremely powerful in enhancing health. Bartering, giving in order to get something back in return, does not give the same results. Collectively these studies prove that giving, far more than receiving, is the most potent force for good on the planet, for acts of personal generosity reverberate through our bodies and across the entire span of our lives, bringing health, healing, and happiness in astonishing ways.

These studies show that giving, far more than receiving, is the most potent force for good. Jesus of Nazareth, who attained the higher Christus consciousness, recognized this when he said, "it is better to give than to receive." This does not make us morally superior, but rather is a practical tool for feeling love and being healthier.

Since the love we give is more important than the love we get, let us choose to make up for the love we didn't get by giving the love we have been withholding from others or seeking outside ourselves for all these years. It is through the giving love that we are reminded that love is already what we are. We cannot give something which we do not have. When we are seeking love, we feel the absence of love, yearning to finally find it somewhere out there. A common practice is to barter for love: "I did this for you, so I expect such and such back in return." As long as we think love is out there, separate and apart from us, we will continue to feel empty and deprived, for we have entered into the illusion that we are separate from love. We think it only resides in the appointed person.

We then feel unloved, depressed, sad, empty and afraid, and all our 50-70 trillion cells respond accordingly. Our arms would become weak in a muscle test. On the other hand, when we think a thought of loving kindness or compassion toward anyone, our hearts reaching out only wanting to help while expecting nothing back in return our arms become very strong along with feeling the deep peace and joy that goes with it, feeling full of abundant love. In extending love in our minds or in our actions we have moved out of our illusion of separateness and the erroneous idea of who and what we are. Since we cannot give something we do not have, extending love is a reminder of who we are at the Core. And even if some people don't get that giving is its own reward, they will still feel the helpers high, which also reverberates throughout our cells.

We must remember to be careful, however. If the love turns into wishing for something back in return, or if we are doing it to live up to an image of a good loving person or to be a good Christian or Buddhist it is likely to drain you instead and make you sick, for you have then dis-identified with love. You have shifted to try to be something you are supposed to be, rather than just being love itself, which you are.

Forgiveness: Blessing People Who Have Given Us Challenges

What happens when we encounter or live with a very difficult and challenging person? How can we remain at peace and keep our cells at peace to keep away dis-ease? We know that if we cannot remain at peace, we become resentful, overwhelmed, depressed and we get sick. Or we may choose to leave.

But whether or not we stay or leave, there is another option. We can give thanks for them and bless them, for they have provided us with an amazing opportunity to learn that love is inside us all the time. We are never separate from Love. If we can then see the deep fear or pain which is always underneath the surface of anyone being difficult, it gives us an opportunity to extend love and compassion, and to remember Who We Really Are!! It has provided us with an opportunity to transcend that which is negative around us and <u>not be a victim of it.</u> And if we can learn that with this person, how much that will benefit us when we have to face the next more difficult and challenging person or situation. And all of this reverberates through our bodies.

Another study carried at the Heartmath Institute has shown that the electromagnetic field of the heart can be measured up to three meters from the body. They say it probably reaches further, but that we just do not have the instruments to measure it yet. They have found, therefore, that when one is loving, we have a coherent heart rhythm. We can have a clearly positive effect on others around us. Conversely, if we harbor negative emotions, we can have a negative effect on others. Consequently, we strongly influence and affect our environment either way, and then our environment effects us back in turn. This is one more indicator that we are not powerless, but help to create our world through what we feel in our bodies and the world about us.

One of the Tibetan monks who was imprisoned by the Chinese Communists and kept in solitary confinement and tortured was a friend of the Dali Lama. After he was released, the two of them were having a conversation one day, and the Dali Lama asked the monk: "When you were imprisoned and tortured, what was your biggest challenge?" The monk reflected silently and then replied, "Well, there was one day . . . when I almost let myself feel hatred for my perpetrators." He had learned the way not to feel like a victim, in spite of horrendous external circumstances, and to keep his mind on forgiveness and compassion—the major source of strength and power. He had remembered his True Self identity.

Please consider the following tool to help lead you into forgiveness, a key to happiness and health:

The Practice of Forgiveness

When we hold onto resentment or have difficulty forgiving those who have hurt us, we unwittingly disturb our peace of mind and heart. Our body's cells are then disturbed or upset. Our ego mind is often invested in such a lack of forgiveness, convincing us that it's fair or understandable to feel anger or resentment toward those who have hurt us. However, not forgiving only keeps us miserable, while the perpetrator may well be enjoying a day on the beach. Essentially, as described above, forgiveness is simply a release mechanism from our own suffering, which comes from consciously deciding not to hold onto resentment—essentially a decision to choose inner peace.

Forgiveness is not condoning what harm someone has done to us. Forgiveness does not mean you are letting someone off the hook for hurting or betraying you. Nor is forgiveness a pardoning of the sinner. True forgiveness starts with benefits for YOU. It is a mechanism for releasing you from your own grievance, which in turn is causing you resentment, fear, pain, and stress. If you become free of your own disturbance, then you help to heal yourself from your suffering—and in doing so, you help to heal the world. I now give thanks for the people who have been most challenging in my life, for they actually helped me grow far more than if they had not been there. Norman Cousins put it beautifully when he said, "Life is an adventure in forgiveness, for there is no shortage of people for us to forgive."

One reason the Tibetan monks showed no sign of PTSD, even when they had been tortured except when kept in solitary confinement by the Communists authorities for years, was that they carried no resentment. What saved them from being emotionally damaged was their ability to continually extend forgiveness toward their captors.

Forgiveness, therefore, is not for someone else: it is your path to happiness and health. It enables your body to be healthy. It is our road to peace and health. Did withholding forgiveness ever change anyone for the better anyway? In fact, not forgiving always adds to our own suffering!

The Value of Our Challenges

I did not learn to snow ski until after I was an adult and went to New England for graduate school. For years, I was an OK skier, but would feel great fear when I encountered a difficult black diamond trail. I could feel the stress hormones surging, my whole body tense, feeling frightened for my survival. I then went for a solid week of ski lessons in Colorado. At first, our instructor helped us unlearn bad habits or faulty techniques. Then he taught us new skills and began to take us to more and more difficult terrain, challenging us to improve our skills. By the end of the week I was skiing black diamond trails with considerable comfort, confidence, and often fun. I believe that the same is true about the rest of our lives. As philosopher Frederick Neitzche quoted it from Alexander the Great, "That which doesn't kill us can make us stronger." We do not have to stay stuck with our challenges overwhelming us, for we can diligently practice the tools in this book, all of which are tools I consistently practice on myself and will do so the rest of my life. As we continue our practice of these tools, we begin to feel more and more of our own inner Strength. When we feel inner strength, our stress hormones quiet down and we find it easier to stay healthier.

Instead of seeking for all the love you missed for so long in your life: GIVE IT!

If your self talk has been negative, use the tools here to CHANGE IT!

So what if you have had traumas and other painful experiences in your past: CLEAR THEM!

If you having negative emotions wanting them to linger: focus on them, feel them, and then do a thymus/heart rub to LET THEM GO!

So what if you have difficult people to deal with in your life: BLESS THEM AND SEND THEM LOVING COMPASSION!

So what if you have been sick for years: YOU CAN HEAL!

We do not need to remain victims of our past and keep making ourselves sick! We can remember that we are Love itself thereby making ourselves strong, extending love everywhere we can. It is first and foremost a gift to ourselves, making us happier and healthier as well as making our mindbodies stronger. And then what we give to ourselves automatically spills over to everyone around us and out to even unknown numbers of people. What we give to others, we give to ourselves, and what we give to ourselves, we give to others.

CHAPTER 9

Becoming Mindful of Body Sensations and Thoughts

❧

God is more completely expressed
through the man who lives largely
than through the one who lives meagerly.
The Science of Mind

Many of us are rarely mindful of our body sensations or our thoughts until they are screaming loudly. Or if we are aware of body sensations, we will give a quick answer implying an external cause, for our ego minds will want us to be powerless victims by viewing it this way, and we will rush to a doctor to fix it. Or the ego mind will stop us from learning from our mindfulness by making us feel guilty for identifying an underlying cause. So many people have been unable to help themselves because they take these explorations as blaming the victim, which is why you are reminded so often and repeatedly in this book. Our goal can never be to blame ourselves or anyone else since it only creates more of a problem, including more sickness. Instead, we just need to be eternally curious as to what our body sensations are saying, and attend to these messages with compassion, love and understanding, for those are the mental and healing energies.

You will need to treat any sensation in the body, especially a pain, as a language to be translated. Our job is not to make it go away or run quickly to the doctor to take it away for us. However, if you believe enough that the doctor can take it away, it will probably work, at least for the time being. But let's not stop there and miss the more important learning which will keep us healthy and happy because we have identified and translated the language. Now we can deal with the source of the problem with a new decision.

Reading the Body's Language: A Tool

To read your own body language, first sit quietly and reflect. (If you are having an acute emergency situation, then go to the emergency room first.) Otherwise, it is often far more helpful to get in touch with the messages your body is trying to communicate to you. Do the process very slowly.

1. **Sit in a comfortable place, preferably a quiet one, so that you can focus.**

2. **Take a number of slow and deep breaths, first exhaling fully, and then inhaling when your body needs oxygen.**

3. **Inhale through your nose with your tongue behind your front upper teeth, and exhale through slightly pursed lips.**

4. Focus on any sensations or symptoms you are readily aware of.

5. Notice what the sensation or symptom does just because you focus on it without judging or trying to change it (while continuing to breathe). Does it get stronger or weaker? Does it move or stay in the same place?

6. Ask yourself, "What is my body trying to tell me here?" It is important to think of it as language needing to be translated. Allow any seemingly irrational or remote answers to come into your mind. Make a mental or written note about them.

7. Once you have your answers to a particular body sensation or symptom, take your focus to another one of which you are aware and repeat the same process.

8. Once you have attended to any sensations that are in your awareness, begin to scan your entire body, starting at your feet and slowly moving upward, checking in attentively with each little part of your body. Any time you discover another sensation, repeat the above process of focusing on the sensation without judgment or trying to change it, but just being curious to decipher the message your body is giving you.

9. Now begin the same kind of mindfulness of the thoughts that are going through your mind.

10. Notice what each thought makes you feel— either an emotion or a sensation in your body.

11. Are you thinking thoughts that bring you peace and joy, or are they thoughts which create worry, fear, resentment, guilt, or anger?

12. Are you thinking thoughts of judgment about yourself, others, or anything going on in the world? Or are you thinking thoughts of acceptance, forgiveness, compassion and joy? How does each thought make you feel in your body?

13. Essentially, do your thoughts make you feel good or do they make you feel bad? Observe how each kind of thoughts make you feel in your mindbody.

14. About each sensation, remember to ask yourself what is my body trying to say to me? Since your body is your subconscious mind, deciphering its language helps to make its language conscious where you can attend to it.

Doing this exercise for a while will help you to become more conscious of your body language and your negative thoughts on a daily basis which alone can help you be healthy and happy. It will also help you become more able to use the practices which follow much more effectively.

ALTERNATIVE: (You may choose to be guided through this process by listening to the downloaded instructions at www.henrygrayson.com. Just close your eyes and hear the voice guiding you through each of the above steps.)

Translating your Body Language

Once you identify the symptoms or sensations in your body, you then need to translate the language. Tom's "shoulder had given him problems" off and on for years. In order to determine what was causing his shoulder to give him problems, he had gone to doctors, deep-muscle massage therapists, chiropractors, a homeopathic physician, and taken muscle relaxants. Then he tried acupuncture, which energy balancing helped temporarily in relieving his painful symptoms, but the pain "kept coming back." Since Tom truly thought it was the shoulder which was giving him the problem, he sought out help from these diverse practitioners to fix the shoulder "which was killing him." His pain had the power to come back. Tom had projected all his power onto the shoulder, saw it as being the source of pain possessed with the willful intent to harm him, as revealed in the common language which we ordinarily overlook. Tom began to understand that his body had not willed to harm him and his shoulder could not will to give him problems. In fact, it had no power to will at all. Only then did he begin to take back his power to heal. It was just a part of his own mind, the egoic thought system, which was speaking through his body and he had not known how to translate the language his body was using. If we do not translate the body's language we will go down a dead-end street in our attempt to solve the problem, and often suffer needlessly, since it is likely to keep occurring.

Since childhood, Tom had felt a need to take care of his mother, who was often ill. Being the oldest, she also often made him responsible for his two younger siblings as well. Every afternoon after school, he had to take care of them at home while his friends were playing ball in the street in front of his house. From this developmental trauma of being deprived of nurturance himself, and at the same time having to take care of everyone else, he had developed a belief that I don't deserve to be taken care of. An outgrowth of this belief was another of significance: "I can only get love if I carry everyone else's burdens," which his shoulder was doing. It was literally burdened down.

Let us remember for a moment that Einstein said that it was "an optical illusion that we are separate." What could confirm that optical illusion more than our inhabiting separate bodies? Given that we all mostly live in that illusion, when we see a bunch of separate bodies, it is very hard for most of us to believe that we are interconnected at an invisible level. It is living in this illusion of separateness that makes us feel little and powerless at the effect of others, of circumstances, and even of parts of our bodies. We feel victimized, separated from love, separated from our awareness of our capacity to create in every area of our lives, and make our bodies an expression of some of the unconscious mind. It is here that we can see that what our body says takes on greater importance.

If the body is the home of the egoic mind, part of the illusion of separateness, then most of the body's communications are an attempt to keep us in the illusion that we are separate and keep our interconnectedness unconscious. But on the other hand, we can take what the egoic mind uses to keep us distracted by pain and fear, and perform a spiritual alchemy. We can take the body's communications and use them, not as a distraction, but as a way of identifying the egoic voice, seeing it for what it is, and then transcending it so that it has no negative effects on us whatsoever, including painful bodily symptoms. We can turn the lead into gold. Certainly, we can use the body for much joy, peace, and as expressions of great love. This is one of our highest goals. But the false-self mind will always oppose these. So let us use every sensation or symptom in the body to help identify this egoic mind. If we can begin to translate our body's language, then we can attend to the egoic message before it takes us away from our loving, joyful, and powerfully creative nature. Therefore, in the case of physical symptoms, we can begin to listen to the little signals and attend to them before they become huge ones.

Remember our analogy of driving down an interstate highway: There are little grooves or markers on the side of the road to call our attention to the fact that we are starting to run off the road. If we have dozed, spaced out, or been distracted, the sound and vibration of those little markers wakes us up to focus on where we are going. If we do not heed that little warning, we may run off the road onto the shoulder. If that does not wake us up, we can run into a ditch. If that does not work to get us awake, we might crash into a tree, our run off a huge cliff. So it is with our body symptoms. If we listen to the little signals and attend to them in a positive and constructive way, then we may well avoid a heart attack, cancer, diabetes, or other serious illness farther down the road. Most often these illnesses do not just erupt out of the blue, as is much of our common thinking. They have been germinating out of the jittery or depressed cells for weeks, months and often years. And this germination started in the mind.

Most people will be concerned when they hear a strange noise in their automobile, and attempt to find out what is going on. But they take their little muscle tension, colds and sore throats, stomach problems, skin rashes, back pains, or headaches as the common way of living in the world. Or they treat these symptoms as they would their auto, by taking it to a repair shop to be fixed by the mechanic. We need to do something much more important than getting our body part fixed quickly, although that is OK, too. We also need to remember that the conflict expressed in those little symptoms, when not attended to, can easily grow and become fertile soil for greater problems, physical, spiritual, and emotional.

Through large parts of every day, most of us are ruled by the egoic part of our minds, often called through the centuries the great deceiver or the wolf in sheep's clothing. The exceptions are those moments when we love purely, are free of fear and worry, are in total peace and joy, and trust our capacity to create our lives as we want them to be. To the extent that we are not totally joyful and at peace, and not creating the life we want, we need to identify the egoic voice for what it is and use one of the tools in this book for letting it go. Reading the body language can help immensely to identify this voice as a starting point.

Ways to Read the Body's Language

1. Practicing Mindfulness:

Breathe: If we stop, sit quietly, and focus on the breath, we will begin to relax. When the egoic mind if full of chatter, it is harder to get any other kind of message, let alone do a translation. So we need to begin by becoming mindful. Mindfulness is being aware of whatever is most salient and dominant in our field of awareness, and then gradually expanding our field of awareness.

* Start by just observing how your breath is occurring. Take your time without hurrying.

* Is your breath fast or slow?

* Is it shallow or deep? Try not to judge it our change it. Just observe it. After you have been mindful of your breath for a few moments, then . . .

* Observe any sensations in your body.

* Are any of these sensations uncomfortable?

* Are there any places where you feel tension or tightness in your muscles?

* Are you aware of needing to adjust your posture? Feel free to do so.

* Do you feel pain anywhere?

* Do you feel itching anywhere?

* Do you feel or hear any activity in your digestive system?

* Are you aware of your heart beat?

* Are you aware of wanting to rush through the exercise?

Focus on any and all of these sensations as you continue to breathe.

Say to yourself: "I wonder what this sensation or pain is trying to tell me."

Pause thoughtfully. See what just pops into your mind. Consider it even if it seems irrational.

If your body sensation could speak in the 1st person, how would it complete these sentences?

I feel _____

I really want _____

I'm afraid _____

If only _____

I wish _____

I'm angry at _____

Because _____

I'm sad that _____

I'm worried that _____

I'm guilty about _____

I resent _____

I don't want _____

I would most like _____

Consider Jack, whose back would go into spasm several times a year, keeping him from going to work to the dismay of his employer. As he breathed and relaxed as guided above, he then began to fill in the above blanks as follows:

I feel tired, *"exhausted and in pain"* _____

What I really want is *"rest"* _____

I'm afraid *"I will be a slave for the rest of my life"* _____

I wish I could *"find a less demanding job"* _____

I am sad because *"I have had to work so hard"*

I am angry with my father because _"he pressured me to be working at something all the time"_

I'm worried _"that I am stuck"_

I'm guilty about _"not working longer hours. What I do is never enough"_

I resent _"my father for putting all that pressure on me to work at what I don't like, just because it is a good profession to make money"_

I don't want _"this back problem any longer"_

I would most like _"to be healthy and happy in my career"_

The theme for Jack is quite obvious. Due to pressure from his early experience with his father, he developed several belief systems: (1) that he has to work hard or he will lose love and approval; (2) that his work has to be a "good" profession whether he likes it or not; (3) that he never does enough, no matter how much it is; and (4) he was not free to make other choices.

No matter how many health practitioners Jack sees, it is not likely that he will be free of his recurring back problem until he clears out the trauma of his father's pressure and demands, and clears each of those negative beliefs which grew out of that trauma of pressure.

Once Jack clears his trauma and negative core beliefs, almost any intervention will probably work, because he will not have to use the back pain to try to change his life for him but at a great and painful price. Once again, the egoic mind's solution is to stay attached to back pain, but this will clearly produce more of a problem. By identifying the real communication in his body, he also shifts the locus of power from outside to inside where his True Power lies. Now he can truly have an effect on solving his back problem by solving his emotional conflict. He can use his body to heal his mind which needed his body to be sick as a solution to his problem. This now allows his body to be healed as a fringe benefit because he no longer believes that the egoic mind's solution is the only one available to him.

Dialogue With Your Body Technique

1. Once you have identified sensations or pains in your body, focus on that place for a moment to truly feel it. Then, consider it as an entity which you would like to dialogue with.

2. Decide what you would like to say to or ask your pain or body sensation.

3. Make the statement or ask your question as if your body sensation were a person sitting with you. Do it aloud.

4. Let the body sensation reply to you, using your mouth to speak its answer aloud to you. This may seem a little strange at first, but with a little practice it can often reveal some very helpful answers. The egoic mind, however, would like you to be too uncomfortable to use this process, telling you it is too weird, so you will stop doing it and therefore not

get to your answers which could lead you to more health, happiness and success. Do not let it rule you any longer, because you do have a choice.

5. Then allow yourself to respond to what the body sensation or symptom said.

6. Next, give your reply again.

Continue this dialogue as long as needed to reach a resolution that you consider different from the one you started with, and one which gives other answers to the problem.

Example of Voice Dialogue

Here is an example of dialogue with the self. Note what Christina, who had an overly stressed adrenal gland resulting in an adrenal deficiency, did with this dialogue process.

> **Christina** (to her adrenal gland): "What the hell are you doing, over working so much as to almost wear yourself out and me along with it?"
> **Adrenal gland:** "I'm sorry. I was just trying to protect you. You have had so many traumas in your life especially as a child. You needed the extra adrenaline to be safe."
> **Christina:** "Yes, but I'm experiencing everything as not safe now—even things that most people totally trust to be safe. I feel like I'm living on adrenaline."

Adrenal gland: "What do you want me to do? I was just trying to help."

Christina: "I would like you to ease up. I'm going to clear out the effects of those traumas so you can relax and then I can relax. Let's work together to relax and save some of that adrenaline for when I really need it."

Adrenal gland: "OK, but you will have to show me how."

This dialogue came after Christina had recognized why her adrenals had worked overtime, and she was already poised to begin her process of clearing out the effects of her ongoing developmental traumas which seemed to have gone on endlessly in her original family.

So, before you rush to simply eradicate a physical symptom, be curious about your body language and what it is saying. When you can attend to its language from your higher Self instead of from the egoic mind, your symptom will often go away. Do not be dismayed if it sometimes does not happen quickly. This is not an occasion to feel guilty, but instead continue to be patient and curious. Always be kind, patient and loving with your self never blaming or creating guilt!

Use your body to heal your mind that needed your body to be sick. This is the healing of the TRUE SELF.

CHAPTER 10

Rituals for Self Healing

You are where your thoughts are.
So be sure that where your thoughts are is where
you want to be.
Rebbi Nachman of Breslow (1790)

Once we have cleared all our barriers to healing, it is all too easy to let our thoughts fall back into an old pattern of not holding our consciousness in support of happiness, health, and healing. Even though we may have removed that which held us back, the ego mind likes us to use the problems or sensations in the body to pull us into what seems in the present to be wrong or not functioning well, instead of allowing us to become truly healthy from moment to moment. This part of our minds will try relentlessly to have us give up our power with even such a simple thought as my back is bothering me today, or my neck is killing me, again projecting our power onto our backs or necks as if they had intention to harm us.

We are victims primarily of our own thoughts and perceptions. But even those we have the power to change. I will always remember Victor Frankl's conclusion in my seminar with him in graduate school: "even when all our human freedoms are stripped away as in a Nazi concentration camp, there is one freedom those Nazi guards could not take away from us. It is the freedom to choose what we think in our minds!"

We can so easily let our thoughts slip into themes of helplessness, despair, and hopelessness. In doing so, we are sending the opposite messages to our body's cells, telling our body to take in illness instead of health and happiness.

It is here that healing rituals can be of great value. Rituals are essentially a way of giving heightened focus of conscious intention, whether educational, religious, political, or for healing. They can harness our positive thoughts while keeping out the opposing negative thoughts. By engaging in such mindful healing rituals, we take back out intrinsic power by consciously creating health and healing.

Since our survival brain is so much more programmed to the negative, the conscious use of healing rituals can give us support to override the negative thoughts and positively instruct our bodies to embrace health and happiness. It is through projection that we disown our power, and then attribute that power to a body part or to some thing or some one external. *A Course in Miracles* states it thus: "You see what you believe is there, and you believe it is there because you want it there." But it is likely that the part of us that expresses much of our wanting is not in our awareness. Much of what we manifest is what our ego mind wants when we allow it to be out of conscious control. And this part of our minds wants to keep us in the illusion of separation, therefore in powerlessness, victimization, pain, suffering, and deprivation.

Healing rituals can counter these messages. If we look at what we are manifesting, or what we are experiencing, perhaps we can get a clearer idea of what is going on inside us, contributing to our outer experience—or the experience in our bodies. Now we are becoming more conscious.

When, for example, there is a problem with our digestion, in the ego mind we may focus totally on the disturbance we feel in our stomachs or bowels just feeling the pain, or we focus on how something outside has caused the problem (virus, a food, etc.). In doing so, we project our power to something external and thereby intensify and often prolong the problem. If there is a back pain, we think, act and move as if we are incapacitated, which only perpetuates the problem. If we are going for chemotherapy as cancer treatment, we are likely to focus on the diagnosis with fear, or we are severely distracted by the adverse reactions to the chemotherapy which makes us even sicker. *These are times we most need a way to hold our consciousness on health and healing instead of focusing on what is wrong no matter how strong the pain, for what we focus on and how we interpret it is much more than an observation of a fact. It is an act of creation.* Meaningfully constructed rituals can help us keep that focus, thereby opening new neural pathways and the increased flow of positive instruction to your body.

Some Personal Healing Rituals I Have Used

I'd like to share some of the rituals I have used for healing or for sustaining my health. But we must remember that these rituals are not the true healing. Instead, they are tools that helped me to focus my conscious mind and direct my energy toward healing instead of having my mind support sickness and suffering with its automatic thoughts which have long been programmed. Yes, I used them to heal my body. But more importantly, they were steps in healing my mind, the more basic and greater healing, as I took back the internal Power of my true Self.

Most important, it is my hope that the rituals I have used for diverse forms of healing will inspire you to think creatively about rituals you might use to hold your healing and health consciousness. It is important that the primary purpose is not to heal the body, but to heal the mind that needed the body to be sick. Then, most often, the body just falls in line. The ritual is to assist us in focusing our minds, taking back the power of our thoughts, and reclaiming our immense Creative power by sending different messages to our cells. While you might choose to use one similar to what I have used, it is even more valuable for you to develop your own rituals which fit you and your particular dis-ease. Let the healing rituals listed below which I have used inspire you to develop your own.

My Vitamin and Herbal Ritual

I take a number of vitamins, minerals and herbs as a part of my daily health ritual. While there are probably intrinsic benefits from each of the things I ingest, I believe that the greatest value is in the ritual I use when taking them which helps me harness the powerful placebo effect (my positive belief in what they can do being the strongest healing agent). I use a small bathroom paper cup to put all of my supplements in before I swallow them. As I open each jar and place the pill or capsule into the cup, I have a quick thought about what each is doing for me in a positive way. For example, I think of the vitamin E as keeping my arteries open and healthy. I think of the various antioxidants as keeping all the contaminants and pollutants cleared out of my body. I think of the CO Q-10 as enhancing a healthy heart. I think of the saw palmetto as helping to keep my prostate healthy. I then think of the vinpocetine and the phosphatidylserene as working to sustain outstanding memory and mental functioning, while at the same time I am careful not to think or talk about how I might not be remembering things I used to remember—for example, remembering that what we focus on we will get more of.

The studies in the psychology of perception by Wilheim Wundt in the 1800's pointed out that what we focus on becomes the figure, while other things in our perception recede into the ground. The figure becomes more of our reality in front of us. If we focus on one corner of a room where the paint is soiled or damaged, we do not see all the beautiful art work hanging on the walls. On the other hand, if we focus on the art, the soiled paint recedes way into the background. We literally create different personal realities moment by moment, depending on where we focus.

This ritual with my supplements, therefore, keeps me focused on a variety of ways I am sustaining or creating health, whereas I might not have any such thoughts, not only as I take my supplements, but also as I go about my activities throughout the day. Without the ritual I might not focus on such positive thoughts at all as they could fade into the background. But if I use this ritual to harness the placebo effect, I get far more than my money's worth from the supplements. In doing this ritual I am telling my body what to do repeatedly each day and how it is going to stay healthy. It is possible that I could be getting several times the intrinsic value of the supplements through this ritual.

Healing a Bone Spur

A number of years ago, I had grown a bone spur on my heel which the doctor said would need to be removed surgically. But my choice was to do self healing work first, and consider invasive, costly, and painful procedures such as surgery only as a last resort, unless it was an urgent necessity. After taking care of the answers to My Six Questions, and identifying issues I committed myself to attend to differently, I then decided to come up with a ritual to promote the healing of my bone spur. In fact, it took me several weeks before I could come up with a ritual which seemed to really fit and which I could believe in. One day as I was walking around my carpeted bedroom while getting dressed, I became acutely aware of the wonderful feeling of the soft carpet under my feet, and realized I had found my ritual. Since my exercise routine includes considerable fast walking several times each week, I decided I could do some of that walking in my bare feet in my bedroom. As I walked I would imagine how my bare feet on the carpet would help all the little bones in my bare feet to move about easily, far better than they could strapped into a shoe. I thought of this as increasing the blood flow throughout my foot and beginning to take away the calcification of the bone spur. Doing this exercise 5-10 minutes a day with my focus on what it was doing for me, the bone spur starting to shrink, and it was fully gone in a couple of months without surgery.

The healing did not come from the exercise. While I might have received some linear benefit from walking on my carpet, I believe the greatest benefit came from how I instructed my body to use the exercise. We must remember that our bodies with the 50-70 trillion cells are like little soldiers following orders. And then, the greater healing was in my remembering the power of my own mind, remembering who and what I truly am.

Healing a 2nd Degree Burn

About thirty years ago, I was driving around Manhattan where I lived at the time to pick up several colleagues to drive to a seminar in Westchester County, just north of the city. At that time I had one of those old 12 cylinder Jaguars which was known for overheating in hot weather, which is what happened that day. I opened the hood to allow more air to circulate around the engine, and as I looked closely the radiator hose exploded in my face, burning the entire right side of my face, ear and head, barely missing my eye. My friends rushed me to New York Hospital, where I waited on a gurney in the emergency ward for 2-3 hours for treatment, the pain getting worse by the minute.

While lying there, I remembered a story a patient had told me the week before about a friend of hers who had an appendectomy scar that she wanted to eradicate, since she liked to wear bikinis in the summer at the beach. She had done deep breathing, breathing into the scar as she inhaled, and as she exhaled she imagined it was taking away the scar tissue. Apparently she had been about 90-95% successful at that point. I thought, if she could do that for a two-year-old scar, what might I be able to do for a fresh burn? So I began to breathe into my burn, imagining that the air was swirling around in the burn, taking away the pain and any infection as I exhaled. Then I realized that I was breathing in New York City pollution, so in order to purify the air, I imagined that the air was going through the hairs in my nostrils which would serve as a purification system, thereby sending clean air into my burn. Within 3-4 minutes most of my pain had disappeared. I continued to do this for a couple of hours until I could be examined by a physician in the emergency room, who declared that I indeed had a 2nd degree burn. He insisted that I take morphine tablets home, saying that I would be in such intense pain in the evening and that I would feel like shooting him if I did not have pain medication to use. I filled the prescription and took the painkillers home, but never had to take them as I continued to do my breathing and visualization, which were working beautifully, imagining my face to be healing quickly and completely while breathing out the pain. When I went back to see the doctor for the follow-up visit a few days later, he exclaimed that I was healing about twice as fast as was normal, saying, "I don't know what you are doing. Don't tell me what it is cause I probably won't believe it. But keep doing whatever it is!" The scabs disappeared and I healed fully with no scar in only one week.

But I must ask: Was the true healing the healing of my 2nd degree burn in record time with no scars? No. Of course I totally welcomed it. But the true healing came from reconnecting with my inner Divine Power. I simply used the ritual as a means to recognize and embrace the power of consciousness that was already within. The physical healing was just the highly welcomed fringe benefit.

Relaxing Painful and Tight Muscles

If I start to do a yoga stretch and discover I have a tight muscle somewhere in my body, my old way was to favor it and to avoid stretching that particular muscle until the tightness was gone. The other even older way was to force myself to push through the tightness to work it out, following the foolish adage: "no pain, no gain." I usually hurt myself following this, the ego's way. Now, I do neither of these. Instead, when I feel muscle tightness, I first ask myself, what is being expressed there? Is it an emotion I have not been dealing with consciously? Is it serving some other need or function I have not consciously attended to? Once those answers have been attended to, I then imagine as I stretch that the stretching motion is taking out the tension that very moment in the act of doing the exercise, including relaxing the muscle and taking away any pain that had been there. I find the minute I shift my thoughts, purely instructing in this direction, the pain ceases and the muscle stretches successfully and easily immediately. In essence, I tell the muscle and nerves what to do.

Healing Hemorrhoids

Several decades ago I went to a surgeon since I had developed a case of hemorrhoids. After he had examined me, he said to me with a pleasurable grin on his face, classically Freudian for a surgeon: "I think we need to cut them out. Would next Wednesday work for you?" I paused for a couple of minutes, remembering something I had recently read in a health newsletter about hemorrhoids that they could come about from too much sitting without enough exercise, which is certainly what I had been doing at that time since I sit so many hours doing psychotherapy sessions. I had also read that a magnesium deficiency might show up in a hemorrhoid problem. I told him that I would think about the surgery as a back-up measure, but that I was going to do more exercise and take magnesium first. His face drooped sadly as I walked out of his office. Using the ritual of focusing on how my hemorrhoids would heal while I exercised and as I ingested my magnesium, I totally healed them in a couple of months. I continued to keep exercise in my lifestyle and magnesium in my consumption, and have had no recurrence of the problem since keeping thoughts of abundant health. The ritual helped to show me that the mind, not the body has the power to rule, and reminded me of some yogis who have been known to heal a deep cut or a burn completely within a few minutes, even though it took me longer.

Healing Severe Pain

A number of years ago I had my first root canal done a day before leaving on vacation. The next day, my family and I were driving across the state of Massachusetts en route to a lake in the White Mountains of New Hampshire where we were going to vacation. Suddenly, I felt a severe pain in my jaw, feeling as if I had been shot that instant! I screamed out in pain, which alarmed my family, for I am not one to complain about pain. But the suddenness and severity was a big shock to me before I realized that my car windows were intact and that it was my tooth. We were far from any town or drug store, so any kind of pain medication was totally out of the question for at least another 30-45 minutes. Surprisingly, out of the mouth of my five-year-old son in the back seat came the words: "Dad, why don't you breathe?" I was amazed to hear such words of wisdom out of the mouth of such a young child. I had been so totally preoccupied with the sudden pain that I had forgotten that I could breathe.

I began to breathe into the pain, imagine that the air was swirling around the tooth with the pain, releasing any infection. Then, as I exhaled I imagined that I was spewing out both the pain and infection. Within 2-3 minutes I was 98% pain free. After about a half hour I had the thought, "Boy! That was some pain I had!"

With this thought the pain returned instantly! But this time I remembered to return to breathing along with the imagery and instructions about what to do, and once again the pain disappeared. I continued to do this even as I went to bed, even though I had stopped at a drug store to fill a pain medication prescription. I never needed to take the meds, for as long as I remembered to breathe and focus about 95-98% of the pain was gone. I continue to find it amazing to see that while pain is a valuable signal to us and can be incredibly intense; it is also just an illusion which can so easily be vanquished, which is well known in both hypnosis and acupuncture.

Healing a Torn Meniscus Knee Injury

Several years ago I was diagnosed by a prominent sports physician at Mt. Sinai Medical Center in New York City as having a torn meniscus in my knee, resulting from the second of two different skiing injuries. He said that it would need to be repaired surgically. He also added that the injuries had created arthritis in that knee as well, and would need to be scraped out. He declared that the only solution to both was to have surgery to do the repair. I told him I preferred to attempt some self healing first, to see if I would avoid the invasive procedure, and if I was not successful I would be back to see him. He laughed, saying that there was no way I could heal those injuries on my own, but I was welcome to try.

After I had eliminated all possibilities of any need to keep the injury, asking myself My Six Questions, I decided on a multifaceted healing ritual. To clear out the arthritis, I remembered that two elderly aunts of mine had both healed themselves from severe arthritis by taking a tablespoon each of apple cider vinegar and honey in a cup of hot water about two times a day, this being an old Vermont folk remedy. I decided to do that with the instructions to my body to clear out the arthritis as I drank the liquid each day. I was inspired by the study done at the VA hospital in Texas where half the men received the actual surgery for their knees and the other half received sham surgery, only a little incision to look like surgery had taken place. The sham surgery group showed equal results as those receiving the surgery, so why could I not do the same with my belief?

I also decided that I would do gentle exercises during which I would focus on my torn meniscus gradually repairing itself and becoming stronger and healthier each day. Gradually, the pain of the arthritis went away and the looseness in my knee from the torn meniscus healed. I now ski easily without any brace or pain, have no scar on my knee, and I avoided a painful surgery and recovery period. Again, the mind was the ruler of the kingdom of my body.

Healing Skin Cancer

When I was a teenager I spent much time out in the sun with no sun screen since it was rarely used in those days. Growing up near the Gulf of Mexico, I spent many hours doing all sorts of water activities, with long hours in the sun. Even until midlife, I would spend many days on the water with family and friends at my lake house sailing, wind surfing, water skiing, and swimming, or just hanging out by the water socializing. As a result, according to the dermatologist, I had a couple of little basal cell skin cancers, which I allowed him to remove quickly and easily. Of course, he advised me to be much more careful about any excessive sun exposure, which I have followed.

Since then, because of so much earlier damage to my skin, I have had a number of little pre-cancerous crusty growths show up on my face and arms. This time, instead of surgery, I decided to create a ritual to deal with them. I had read about the healing properties of green tea, which gave me the idea for my ritual. Of course, I had already attended to exploring My Six Questions, but for the ritual, I decided I would apply a little green tea extract each morning to the area where the crusty pre-cancerous growth emerged with the thought that the crusty growths would diminish since I had already taken care of any needs to have them. I was amazed to discover that they would disappear within days or a few weeks at the most. Since several more grew up from time to time, I decided to create a little experiment, applying the green tea extract to some and not to others. And as you might expect, the ones disappeared to which I had applied the green tea and given the instruction as to what it was to do. We could debate the question as to whether the result was from the green tea or from the focus of my consciousness while using the green tea. So I applied another ordinary body lotion to the other ones, using the same focus of intent for them to heal as I was using with the green tea, and found that they went away as well, confirming that it was the mind, not the substance, which did the job. In essence, it was the power of the placebo, which is simply the power of my mind.

It would have been easy to feel afraid of the skin cancer and the beginnings of others, if I had allowed myself to follow those thoughts. If I had let myself go into a state of fear, I would have been much more likely to increase the growth of cancer cells. But not falling into fear, but into confidence that I could harness my mind through a ritual, the positive results manifested.

Additional Healing Rituals

Sending Love:

When any part of your body is affected, you might begin to breathe slowly and deeply a few times, and then begin to breathe in love as you inhale; and as you exhale, send love directly to the affected part. Of course, the affected part can be your over-active brain and mind as well as other parts. For example, if you have stomach cramps or other disturbed stomach symptoms, just relax and breathe, breathing love into your heart and sending love to your entire digestive system as you exhale. The more the disturbance, think of how much more it needs love. Continue for several minutes.

Increasing the Placebo Effect:

Whenever you are taking a medicine, whether allopathic, homeopathic, or a natural herb, as you ingest it tell yourself clearly how it will help you heal whatever the problem is. By doing this, you are wading into a new way of thinking, that is, that your thoughts can have a positive effect on your body. You are taking a step to reclaim your power by beginning to believe that your thoughts have power.

Before You Have Surgery:

1. Several days before the surgery begin to do deep breathing, relaxation exercises, or meditation. At the end of your meditation or relaxation, make the following statements to yourself:

   My mindbody is strong and resilient.
   I will respond very positively to the surgery.
   The anesthesiologist will administer just the right amount of anesthesia for my body.
   The surgeon's hands will be extremely skilled and he will make the most helpful decisions.
   I will recover and heal fully in record time in mind and body.

2. Ask the anesthesiologist to read the above statement to you once or twice as you are going under the anesthesia. In case you are embarrassed to ask the anesthesiologist to read the statement, please note that I have heard from numerous patients that their anesthesiologist liked it so much that they asked the patient for a copy of the statement to use with others.
   These statements are clearly suggestions to your psyche. But they are also intentional positive

statements in the doctor's mind as well, helping him or her be more focused.

For Chemotherapy:

When doing chemotherapy, your desire will be to increase the benefits while decreasing other illnesses (side effects). To do this, do a few minutes of deep diaphragmatic breathing, relaxation exercises, or meditation. It will be particularly helpful to breathe in through your nose while holding your tongue behind your front upper teeth. This form of breathing will help to slow down your brain waves to alpha, and sometimes theta, which are slower forms of brain waves where you are more capable of receiving a suggestion than when you are in beta brain waves.

Next, begin to tell yourself that the chemotherapy will go only to the cancer cells while avoiding everything else in your body. Visualize all other parts of your body being protected, therefore greatly reducing the negative effects of the chemotherapy.

Pain-Free Dental Work:

If you are having dental work performed and you would prefer not to have the Novocain then when you sit in the dental chair, begin to breathe slowly and deeply into the diaphragm to keep yourself relaxed. Next, instead of focusing on the painful sensations in your mouth as the dentist works, begin to press your big toe down firmly into your shoe. Feel the sensation in your toe as you press it down and continue to breathe. Breathe and press down with your toe; breathe and press down with your toe. I have found that I reduce about 95% of the pain while doing this process. Dentists have told me in amazement that most people would require significant amounts of Novocain with such procedures. It is the mind that rules. On the other hand, if you focus on how bad the pain is, it is most likely going to increase and intensify.

Annual Physical Exam:

Instead of going to find out what is wrong with me, or harboring the fear that the doctor will find something wrong, I go to the physician's office with an entirely different motive, saying to myself, "I am using the physical health exam to show the doctor and myself how totally healthy I am." Then, the positive results help to support ongoing positive thoughts about my health.

Headache:

Of course, ask yourself the Six Questions first. Then when you have clarified your need for the headache, or what the "headache" is in your life, and make a conscious decision to take care of the issue differently. Instead of running to get an aspirin or ibuprofen, just begin to focus on where you feel the pain as you breathe slowly and deeply and relax. Continue to breathe slowly and deeply. After you have done this a number of times, begin to notice whether the pain seems to increase or decrease; then breathe slowly and deeply. Next, notice whether the pain remains in the same place or moves around at all. Breathe slowly and deeply. Many times people find that just breathing, relaxing and observing the pain and what it is doing rather than fighting it allows it to go away entirely, especially if you have already taken away the cause.

Athletics:

For many years athletic training has embraced visualization as a means of greatly improving skill. A retired army colonel told an amazing personal story when he was speaking at my older son's college graduation. He had been imprisoned by the North Vietnamese and kept in solitary confinement for almost three years. When he was finally released he returned home to Florida and entered a golf tournament the next week and won!

People were amazed, saying, you could not have been in prison! You have been playing golf around the world these years.

"No," he answered. "The way I survived and kept myself sane was to play golf in my mind every day. I would first picture the course I would play. Then I would go up to the first tee and look down the course to the first green. Once I gauged the distance, I selected my club, did my set up carefully, and then imagined myself hitting the ball. I watched where it landed, walked to that place, estimated the distance to the green and selected my next club. I did each step carefully and thoughtfully as if I was on the golf course. This is what kept me from going insane in that solitary confinement."

He played better than if he had been practicing on the course. How could this be? He could picture a perfect golf swing and outcome better than he could actually do it in person. He therefore opened the neural pathways to support an outstanding golf swing rather than practicing one incorrectly.

We can use the same process for keeping health in our mindbodies. The right hemisphere of the brain cannot distinguish between whether something actually happens and our imagination of it happening. In either case it gives off the same messages to our bodies. If we focus on what is wrong, which is the ego mind's natural inclination, the right brain gives that message to our bodies. On the other hand, if we focus on health, it gives forth that message. Studies using PET scans show that people who imagine that they are performing an action activate the same part of the brain that is involved when they actually do that action.

Spend several minutes every day imagining every part of your body as healthy. Imagine that the heart is strong, the arteries are healthily open, and even the valves and electrical system all working together beautifully. For example, you can create a mental picture of the heart pumping blood beautifully throughout the body, bringing nourishment to every cell.

CHAPTER 11

Healing the Illusion of Separateness: A Lifestyle of Love, Forgiveness and Miracles

*A human being is part of the whole that we call
the universe,
A part limited in time and space.
He experiences himself, his thoughts and feelings,
as something separated from the rest a_kind of
optical illusion of his consciousness._
This is a prison for us, restricting us to our
personal desires and to the affection for only the
few people nearest us.
Our task must be to free ourselves from this
prison by widening our circle of compassion
to embrace all living things and all of nature.*
Albert Einstein

Our illusion of separateness must be seen as the basis of all our human suffering and as the greatest barrier to health, healing and happiness. It is behind all negative emotions, for it keeps us in our sense of powerlessness and victimization in so many areas of our lives.

We could not feel lonely and isolated if we did not feel separate. We could not feel little and frail if we did not feel separate. We could not feel angry if we did not feel hurt and afraid, believing our emotional, physical, or our separated ego self survival is at stake. We could not feel anxious or depressed if we did not feel separate or little. We could not feel guilty if we did not feel separate from the All That Is. We could not feel deprived and empty of love if we did not think we were separate from Love. It is all these different expressions of the illusion of separateness that take an enormous toll on our mindbodies, causing us to suffer mentally, physically, and spiritually.

The Golden Rule, "do unto others as you would have them do unto you," is present in all the world's religions and has been recognized as essential to happiness. In essence, it is the universal wisdom of the ages and the recognition that we are all interconnected, and fits together with new conclusions from physicists.

Buddhism: Hurt not others with that which pains your self. *Udanavarga 5.18*

Christianity: Always treat others as you would like them to treat you. *Matthew 7:12*

Confucianism: Do not unto others what you would not they should do unto you. *Analects 15:23*

Hinduism: This is the sum of duty: do nothing to others which if done to you would cause you pain. *Mahabharata 5.1517*

Islam: No one of you is a believer until he loves for his brother what he loves for himself. *Traditions*

Jainism: In happiness and suffering, in joy and grief, we should regard all creatures as we regard our own self, and should therefore refrain from inflicting upon others such injury as would appear undesirable to us if inflicted upon ourselves. *Yogashastra 2.20*

Judaism: What is hurtful to yourself do not do to your fellow man. That is the whole of the Torah. *Talmud*

Sikhism: As you deem yourself, so deem others. Then you will become a partner in heaven. *Kabir*

Taoism: Regard your neighbor's loss as your own loss. *T'ai shang kan ying p'ien*

Interestingly, the *Journal of Spirituality and Health* reported that the golden rule plaque was found on the wall of the Chief of Medicine at New York University Downtown Hospital. He had concluded that if doctors followed The Golden Rule in their interactions with patients, it would encourage respectful and trusting relationships, and says that he has no doubt that relationships affect the success of treatment. The posters now hang in many locations in the hospital and in satellite clinics, and the text can be found it the residents' manual.

In spite of this ancient wisdom and current scientific understandings, it seems necessary that we have a separate identity in order to function in the world. The problem is that we get attached to our individual sense of separateness. Threats to anything we are attached to cause us suffering, which is why the Buddha 2600 years ago recognized that attachments are the basis of our suffering.

Think of the word individuality. If we break it down into its parts: divide or divided in duality that is, divided into duality our need, therefore, is to recognize that we are far, far more than our little individuated selves and that the world of duality is an optical illusion, as Einstein phrased it so insightfully. If, as stated in the creation myth in the Jewish and Christian bibles, we are created in the image and likeness of God, that image and likeness certainly has to be much more than a human body, for God is not an old man sitting upon a cloud in the sky making decisions for or against us. Instead, we have, and are not separated from all the qualities which people have so often projected onto an external flat earth sky god, separate and removed from us. It is the ego mind that is identified with this sense of separateness, and therefore is identified with the body. If we do not realize that we are much more than a body and more than the ego, we will feel separate, and therefore powerless, little, and void of love.

Our bodies, however, are just a symbol of separateness. Remember, they are 99.999% empty space!! Yet there is a greater Self, the aspect of us that is much more than a visible body. It is the aspect that is "the image and likeness of God," for at our very core, we are all the qualities we have denied about ourselves and projected them onto this medieval external flat earth sky god, so separate and removed from who we think we are. But the truth about us is: We are Love itself! We are Creators! We are omnipotent (all powerful)! We are omniscient (all knowing)! We are omnipresent (present everywhere)! But it is not our little ego or false self, nor is it the body which is all these qualities.

But the ego mind wants us to think we are separated from these powerful qualities.

The same perspective is implied in the language of the New Physics as well, for we are seen as an integral part of the Unified Field, not separate and apart from it, since nothing can be apart from it. We are a part of the one mind of the universe, as physicist Irwin Schroedinger put it. It seems that the more advanced scientific theories are essentially concluding what worldwide ancient wisdom has stated for centuries. Both are similar to what transcendentalist Henry David Thoreau recognized when he said: "What lies behind us and what lies before us is nothing in comparison to what lies within us." But even the concept of within and without is somewhat insufficient to explain our interconnectedness, being part of The All. Paradoxically, going within is the recognition that we are connected with everything we think of as out there.

In such a state of identity we do not have to sell ourselves short or listen to the voice of the ego, the false self mind, which would like us to believe we are little, separate, powerless, not worthy or deserving, not safe, and, in particular, believe that we must seek for love from someone out there in order to have love. We do not have to feel like we are victims of our bodies, nor ascribe malicious thoughts to them, but know that it is our minds that rule our bodies. The amazing aspect of who and what we truly are and how we are to live is put succinctly by Robert Wicks in *Snow Falling on Snow:*

> *Liken yourself to a beautiful original part of creation a true work of art.*
> *Then each day ask yourself how you are living: wither in ways that show gratitude for this beauty or in the ways that indicate how you are defacing it.*

In our false self identity, we have also performed another projection as well. We have taken our ego thoughts and the shadow, as psychoanalyst Carl Jung called it, and projected them onto an external evil, sometimes called the devil or Satan, an external evil force, or we simply project this evil onto other people. Yet, what is a shadow but the place where light is blocked? Psychoanalyst Harry Stack Sullivan thought of it as our denying these parts of ourself, thinking of them as "not me." In actuality they are not me because they are not the real me, just being part of the illusory mind. But in order to identify the thoughts and motives of the ego mind, we must first see them as inside us, rather than external, or we will continue to think there is an external power affecting us. Think of how often we believe such statements as "they did it to me," which keeps us locked into a victim mentality. Instead, we can use others as a mirror in order learn about this disturbing part of ourselves, for we have the power to change what is inside us.

As we saw earlier, so much of our sickness is from our tendency to treat our mindbodies lovelessly. We push them relentlessly acting out "no pain, no gain," in so many areas of our lives, not just at the gym. We lay guilt and punishment upon ourselves and tell our mindbodies it's going to get sick: (i.e. "I'm coming down with one of those horrible colds that's going around," or "I know I will die like my father did at 55 years of age from a heart attack.") We hold resentments, deprive our bodies of rest and sleep, deprive them of exercise or over exercise them, feed them polluted junk fuel, harbor anger, judge ourselves relentlessly, often demanding perfection of some kind, use addictions to relieve our stress, bemoan the past and worry about the future, *and then we wonder why we get sick in mind or in body.* In this sense we are defacing this beautiful work of art as well as denying that we are Love itself. Once we conclude that there has to be a better way than the one that has brought me illness, unhappiness and deprivation, then we can be open to a new way of living and being.

A Lifestyle of Love and Miracles

The reason that miracles are not out of the ordinary, but are the natural order is that we are part of Source, The All That Is. When miracles do not occur, it is because the one thing that has gone wrong is that we have entered into the illusion of separateness. When we are in alignment with Source, we have unlimited potential and unlimited power showing up as synchronicities or things we call miracles. When we forget who and what we truly are, we experience ourselves as little, weak and victims.

In the Disney movie and stage play, *The Lion King,* the young lion is positioned to take over the rulership position as king of the jungle. But he is in fear about his power to take over this role, not being sure about his ability to handle the responsibilities of being the new Lion King. As his father, the Lion King, is preparing his son to receive his crown, he bellows forth his major piece of instruction to his son: REMEMBER WHO YOU ARE! Essentially, this is the message for all of us. We need to re-member who we are. We need to awaken from our sleep of forgetting and re-member, that is, to bring back together our awareness of our True Self identity which has unlimited potential. We need to re-member our phenomenal power to affect things just because we observe them, as the eminent physicist Heisenberg has posited. Even physicist John Wheeler questioned: "Could it be that we bring the whole universe into existence through our consciousness?"

True awakening or awareness, as portrayed in the ancient Vedic science of India understood it, is when we can realize that the one observing, that which is being observed, and the process of observing are all one and the same! There is never a time nor a place where we are separate or powerless. But there are many times we forget what we truly are, being part and parcel of the Power of the Universe itself.

Our True Self identity encompasses our innately intuitive, loving, powerfully creative, spiritual aspects of our beings as well as our connectedness with the entire web of life. This is the essence of what we truly are and enables us to access incredible dimensions of power we did not think possible. In the awareness of this True Self, we do not feel at the effect of circumstances or at the mercy of others. We do not feel at the effect of the germs carried by the person sneezing with a cold sitting next to us, nor are we frightened by the news of the next strain of flu coming our way. We are more concerned with giving love than trying to get love, knowing that it actually makes us incredibly strong. Rather than judging others, we practice forgiveness and acceptance, are able to live in peace even in the midst of conflict. We know that our thoughts are not so much statements of facts, but acts of creation, that transcend time and space, because of Who and What we are. Consider the wisdom in the ancient Chinese proverb:

If you want happiness for an hour take a nap.
If you want happiness for a day go fishing.
If you want happiness for a month get married.
If you want happiness for a year inherit a fortune.
If you want happiness for a lifetime help someone else.
If you want eternal happiness know yourself.

It is not our True Self that ever brings pain and suffering in our mindbodies. Nor is it a punishing external Deity that does it to us. Instead, it is always our illusory mind, the ego. Therefore, it is not the external world that is hell, for we can turn it all into peace and happiness in our minds with our interpretations and our perceptions. The Hindus, the Buddha and Jesus of Nazareth all say we can turn our lives into great joy and bliss, when we let go of our ego wishes and fears, our strong likes and dislikes, our judgments of what should and shouldn't be, and our ideas about what is perfect. We must stop seeking for this joy and peace outside ourselves which is dependent on any thing, person, or circumstance which is external. "Within your own house dwells the treasure of joy; so why do you go begging from door to door," is an old Sufi saying. When we hang on to our illusory thinking, then we create our existential hell in the now moments, much of it going directly into our bodies. It is not wrong to desire happiness, as some people have interpreted religious teachings to mean. The error is the seeking it outside when it is inside.

But we also create a hell for ourselves, not only when listening to this illusory and lying voice, but also when we fight against the ego mind. In fighting against it, we thereby make it real and give it power. Instead we need to see that voice only as the voice of illusion, the great deceiver, essentially a pack of lies, and just give no credence to it. When we see the ridiculousness of that voice, then we can laugh at it, which is the most effective way to disempower it. Consider the difference in the way it feels, for example, when you read and think about these different phrases: "battle against an illness" or "allowing wellness."

We need to be identified with love in order for us to be strong in our mindbodies. Thoughts of anger and fear make our muscles weaker; thoughts of love and compassion make our muscles significantly stronger. In earlier chapters we saw how thoughts of love dramatically changed red blood cells and molecules of water.

As we have seen, studies at the Heartmath Institute in California have shown that the heart, our symbol of love, occupies a more important role in human function than previously known in scientific research. It will respond ahead of the brain in response to frightening stimuli. Even more importantly, when responding to fear-provoking images on a video screen, it will also react even before the computer has selected the fear-provoking image. And as we saw earlier, other research Heartmath scientists have done revealed that DNA actually changed its shape according to the feelings of the researchers. When the researchers FELT gratitude, love, and appreciation, the DNA responded by relaxing and the strands unwound. The length of the DNA became longer. But when the researchers FELT fear, anger, frustration or stress, the DNA responded by tightening up.

It actually became shorter and switched off many of our DNA codes. But most important, the codes were switched back on when the researcher subjects had feelings of love, joy, gratitude, and appreciation. And further, individuals who were trained in having feelings of deep love and compassion could change even more dramatically the shape of their DNA.

And, as cited earlier, one of their later experiments revealed profound results with HIV-positive patients discovering that feelings of love, gratitude and appreciation created 300,000 times the resistance they had without those feelings! And in another experiment they found that consciously experiencing appreciation increases parasympathetic activity change which is beneficial in controlling hypertension. So what is the message to us? No matter what the virus or bacteria may be floating around, in order to stay well keep feelings of joy, love, and gratitude.

A Course in Miracles states that "where there is gratitude, love cannot be far behind." It seems that the two are intertwined. In gratitude we have feelings of fullness which helps us be united with Source or Love itself. When we have feelings of scarcity of love, of joy, of peace, of power, we are disconnected from Source in our minds.

Love and forgiveness seem also to be intertwined. When we hold a grudge or focus on vengeance, it makes us weaker, taking away our joy, but also weakening our immune response. Charlotte Witvliet, a professor of psychology at Hope College in Michigan, compared subjects who rehearsed hurtful memories and nursed grudges with other times when they cultivated empathy and granted forgiveness. Using physiological monitoring devices to measure blood pressure, heart rate, galvanic skin response, and even how they furrowed their eyebrows, the data consistently showed that forgiving behavior resulted in significantly lower levels of physical stress and more positive emotions, while unforgiving behavior resulted in higher levels of physical stress.

The Talmud expresses it metaphorically: "Who takes vengeance or bears a grudge acts like one who, having cut one hand while handling a knife, avenges himself by stabbing the other hand." Essentially, withholding forgiveness is an attack upon our selves, emotionally, physically, and interpersonally. In this way, forgiveness is the key to happiness in mind and body. Why? Because when we are feeling and being love, we are connected with our Divine Nature, which is the true healing.

Kathleen Lawler, Ph.D., researcher and professor at the University of Tennessee, found that harboring feelings of betrayal may be linked to high blood pressure, which can lead to stroke, kidney or heart failure, or even death. In her presentation at the American Psychosomatic Society annual meeting in 2000, she reported that high forgivers, those who forgive easily, had both a lower resting blood pressure than those who held grudges.

There is no question in our minds that both gratitude and forgiveness works miracles in our bodies as well as in our relationships, since gratitude and forgiveness are to be viewed as expressions of love itself. So, whether in our moods, in our bodies, or in our relationships, we can be a miracle worker on a daily basis as we express our love through gratitude and forgiveness, making miracles the natural order for us.

ARE THESE THE ONLY TOOLS I WILL EVER NEED?

Some might say, "I have now identified and cleared most of my traumas and painful experiences. I have identified and cleared my negative beliefs. Does this mean that I will always be healthy and happy now?"

There is a more complex answer than a simple "yes" or "no." If we have cleared our traumas and negative beliefs, we have indeed freed up a huge amount of energy which can allow, not only healing of the body, but also allow more joy, contentment, and peace. It also means that it will be easier to observe and let go of our egoic mind thinking.

But life goes on! And since there is nothing constant in the physical universe but change, as the ancient Greek philosopher Paracelsus noted many centuries ago, we must build into our lives different ways of dealing with these changes. We must also embrace our Power of creation that affects the nature of these changes. Therefore, it is necessary that we integrate into our lifestyle practices, behaviors, and attitudes which support the quality of life we wish to create. Do we want a life of feeling powerless like a victim? Or do we wish to feel like we are in the driver's seat, not only of creating directions and experiences in my life, but also how I react to the challenges which come my way? Do I think that happiness and health are things that happen to me? Or do I now make the choice between heaven or hell each moment in my life?

Given my choice to diminish the periods of hell and my strong desire and commitment to increase the moments of heaven, I have increasingly incorporated many things into my life which support this choice. I did very few of these twenty-five years ago, but have gradually increased a wide variety of things which support my chosen direction. I want inner peace and joy, and it is a high priority. You may already be practicing many of these things, while others may be practicing just a few. Others may have not yet begun to incorporate any of these things into their lives.

I would like to share with you the practices I have incorporated over these 25 years which have made immense differences in my life. I did not start them all at once, but have found increasing value in adding to them as I continue through this life. The ego mind would like you to conclude: "I can't possibly do all these! I'll never get anything else done?" I felt that way at the beginning, too. But I have found with each addition, I get more and more done in less time, with less effort, and at a higher quality. *Because* I am doing these things, I get more done. Those who know me closely often state that they don't know anyone who gets so much done. But I would give most of the credit to these practices I have incorporated into my life which enable me to do most of these things without stress.

I do not wish to present these as the way of life you should adopt. They are meant to be only my example of what I have found extremely valuable, not only in being happier, more content, but also allowing only rarely a very slight illness. Perhaps they will inspire you to begin to add more practices which bring you peace and health. I have found that each addition has increased my desired outcome, and helped me to deal with the challenges and traumas of life with much greater resilience, returning to peace far more quickly than in the earlier years of my life.

1. I have always wanted to reserve time to spend with family and friends, as well as to give myself spaces of "down time." Such time I find nourishing, rejuvenating, and fulfilling—especially when we have open, genuine, and honest communication, as well as fun and times of laughter, all in the context of love. Now, I know that much research supports the idea that all these help us be healthier, less depressed, and live longer.

2. Since I was in graduate school, I have continued to ask myself My Six Questions every time I get a symptom, whether big or small:
   - Why might I need this? And now?
   - What would it get for me?
   - What would it get me out of doing?
   - What emotion could be expressed in this symptom that I have not attended to directly?
   - What is the metaphor being expressed in this symptom?
   - Is there a family or tribal belief being expressed in this symptom?

   As a result of finding different ways of dealing with these issues instead of paying the price of getting sick, I have not gotten a full blown cold or flu or back ache for many decades, and the one time I got pneumonia, I then identified what I needed it for and what it would get for me, which helped me heal much faster.

3. After studying with physicist David Bohm, I began to read many books for the layman about Quantum Physics and the incredible power which lies in the invisible realm, of which we are all a part. This led me to begin to think of myself and the world differently, and what our limitless power and potentialities are.

4. I started the practice of meditation about 25 years ago, first only once a day for a short time, then increasing the length of the meditation to 15-30 minutes because I liked the results I was getting. Then, when I learned that the research showed that practicing it two times a day gave triple benefits, I began to add the second time each day—not because of any "should" or "ought," but because I liked the benefits and wanted to have more of them. I found that it was great in helping me reduce stress, bringing calm after dealing with anything that was disturbing. It helped me stay more centered when dealing with difficult people. The coherence of my heart rate variability became greatly stabilized, or returned it back quickly after an upset, and I was more naturally loving more of the time.

5. Next, I began to be more conscious and knowledgeable about what foods are nutritious or harmful, changed my diet accordingly (but not rigidly or in fear), and learned the value of consistent moderate exercise. I learned ways to give myself the complete rounds of exercise without taking the 2-3 hours to travel to the gym and do it there, knowing

I could then have the time for more things I also wanted to do. I have also embraced about 10-15 minutes of yoga stretching exercises every morning, which makes a huge difference in how and what I feel in my body. If I ever miss a couple of days, I notice a big difference in increased stiffness and sometimes pains in my body.

6. Doing slow and deep breathing into the diaphragm has been immensely helpful first aid measure in reducing stress, tension and worry. If I exhale fully, emptying out all the stale air first, I can then get lungs full of oxygen, helping to calm my limbic brain. If I check in with my breathing throughout the day, especially if I feel any tension at all, and then do my slow deep breathing, I feel significantly better.

7. At about the same time I started studying more spiritual works, such as ***A Course in Miracles,*** Yogananda's Kriya Yoga Program, Buddhist teachings and practices, teaching of Satya Sai Baba, the Bible and other psychospiritual works. All these helped me enormously in beginning to see my self and the world differently, and what works to bring joy and peace, particularly the role of loving compassion and forgiveness of my self and others. I also learned that whatever for I used to judge others, that I have usually done the same thing myself or felt like doing it. Such awareness helps me let go of judgments of others more quickly, seeing them as a mirror of my own psyche. I learned that it is my attachment to

things or people that brings pain. If I free myself of attachment, then I am free to love more purely, for attachment interferes with love.

8. I have learned to be very mindful of my thoughts and how they precede so many of my negative feelings. Catching those negative thoughts of the egoic mind, letting them go, or replacing them with more positive or trusting thoughts, continues to bring me far, far more peace than I had ever known before.

9. And then, when I learned the thymus/heart rub and the ways to stimulate the energy meridians as illustrated in this book, I have removed much more fear, worry, guilt, shame, and anger, as well as negative beliefs about myself or life than I could have ever imagined. And especially, I use one or more of these processes to clear out any current disturbing experience I have had. This is not suppressing the emotion, but instead brings healing love and intention for peace to the healing of the disturbance. And it works far, far better than kvetching with a friend about the disturbance.

10. I have learned that I do not like bringing in more "mind pollution." While I want to be understanding and compassionate with anyone who is suffering, I do not want to jump into the quick sand of commiserating with them. Nor do I like to watch or listen to the 95% negative news shows we now have, nor watch action or violent movies, or talk

with people at length about everything that is wrong with the world. I know that such a focus immediately goes into every cell in my body, affects my health adversely and radiates out to everyone around me.

11. Before I crawl out of bed in the morning, I like to start out my day by setting the tone for the day, by saying the following affirmations about myself, with the emphasis on "I AM," which I borrowed and expanded from the Saint Germain Discourses:
I AM inexhaustible energy.
I AM irresistible divine love.
I AM indestructible and perfect health.
I AM ongoing youth.
I AM invincible protection.
I AM inescapable prosperity . . . .
All because I am part of That which we call God.

Think of how different it would be if I started the day with any opposite thoughts, which so many people do.

12. I like to listen twice as much as I speak, which therefore helps me out of our human narcissism. It makes for deeper and more satisfying connections.

13. And, last but not least, I like to laugh a lot. I like to reach the place where I can laugh about previously heavy and disturbing issues for me. I know that laughter also helps produce the endorphins which

help me and all my cells feel better. It also helps me not to take so many things so seriously.

14. As **A Course in Miracles** states it beautifully: "I choose the joy of God instead of pain." This is our conscious choice each moment.

It is my hope that this list will inspire you to begin to add your positive practices into your life in order to create more peace, joy, health, healing, happiness, and abundance. What else is more important except to know that you are part of The All That Is—and then trust . . . .

What are you already doing or what do you choose to begin now?

SOME DAILY PRACTICES TO CHANGE YOUR BRAIN, HEAL YOUR MINDBODY, BE HAPPY, AND MOST IMPORTANT . . . FIND YOUR TRUE SELF

Place a * by those you now practice regularly. Place an X by those you are choosing to include in your life now.

_____ A daily practice of focusing on feelings of thankfulness and gratitude.

_____ A daily practice of meditation, which is essentially a practice of mind training which keeps us observing, not rehearsing negative thoughts. Twice a day, scheduled in, is three times more beneficial than once a day.

_____ A daily or every other day practice of moderate exercise.

_____ A regular practice of yoga, tai chi or some other form of Stretching, breathing, relaxing, and focusing.

_____ A daily practice of being conscious of and monitoring any negative thoughts

_____ Clear out effects of any traumas or other painful experiences as soon as possible, whether from the distant past or recent past.

_____ Clear out any negative or limiting beliefs which remain uncleared.

_____ Practice opening new neural pathways for new beliefs, attitudes and behaviors.

_____ Be conscious of and relinquish quickly any negative thoughts.

_____ Give yourself adequate sleep and rest, and if you can't sleep, just breathe slowly and deeply.

_____ Begin to read and translate the language of sensations in your body—particularly any symptoms.

_____ Give yourself healthy fuel that is nutritious, foods without harmful additives.

_____ Surrender any and all worries to your internal Higher Power, trusting that you will receive guidance and that the outcome will be for the highest good of all.

_____ Become conscious of your breath, making sure you are breathing slowly and somewhat deeply throughout the day as well as other times of practicing diaphragmatic breathing so you are never oxygen deprived.

_____ Smile frequently to help produce endorphins and joy.

_____ Practice forgiveness, knowing that it is a gift to yourself and your health.

_____ Use the *My Six Questions* any time you get a symptom or painful sensation in your body.

_____ Seek out opportunities to show your love to someone. They will appear at almost every angle. It will make you stronger.

_____ Study some psycho-spiritual work that will help you continue to remember who and what you truly are.

Remember: each of the above practices takes you a step closer to remembering your True Self identity, the true healing.

An Invitation

Have you had success in using any of these tools presented in this book?

- Identifying and Removing barriers to healing

- Changing negative thought patterns

- Removing traumas or changing negative beliefs

- Healing yourself of illness, pain or unhappiness

- Making the shift to the new world view to greater potentiality

We would like you to share your stories on my web site: www.henrygrayson.com to inspire others to use these tools to improve their lives. Most of all you will have the joy and satisfaction of knowing that you helped multitudes of others with your stories.

ABOUT THE AUTHOR

 Dr. Grayson received his Ph.D. from Boston University, prior to which he earned a graduate degree in theology at Emory University. He then earned a Postdoctoral Certificate in Psychoanalysis and Psychotherapy from four years of postdoctoral training at the Postgraduate Center for Mental Health in New York City. At the same time, he was an Assistant and then Associate Professor at the City University of New York. He is the founder and is Chairman Emeritus of the Board of Trustees of the National Institute for the Psychotherapies in New York, a postgraduate local and national psychotherapy training institute chartered by the Board of Regents in New York State. He founded and is Director of the Institute for Spirituality, Science and Psychotherapy and is the Founder and past President of the Association for Spirituality and Psychotherapy, a national membership organization. He also founded and directed The American Eating Disorders Center for 20 years. He was the Resident Psychologist on the Weight Watchers Magazine Show, hosted by Lynn Redgrave and aired 5 times a week nationally on Lifetime Cable and has appeared in the documentaries: "The Truth: The Journey Within" and "The Ultimate Answer: We are all Connected," and numerous Public Television specials.

He is co-author of three professional books: *Three Psychotherapies: A Clinical Comparison, Short Term Approaches to Psychotherapy,* and *Changing Approaches to the Psychotherapies* as well as numerous chapters and articles. He has recorded the best selling 9 ½ hour, 8 CD audio series for Sounds True, *The New Physics of Love: The Power of Mind and Spirit in Relationships* (2000). He is also the author of *Mindful Loving: 10 Practices to Deepen Your Connections* (Gotham Books/The Penguin Group, 2003,) which was featured in Oprah Magazine, is in its twentieth printing, and has been translated into Korean and Russian.

Dr. Grayson integrates diverse psychotherapies with quantum physics, neuropsychology (the new brain scan studies), subtle energies, with Eastern and Western spiritual mindfulness. He has created innovations on the new "power therapies" such as EMDR, Emotional Freedom Techniques (EFT), EFTA), Tapas Acupressure Technique (TAT), and Thought Field Therapy (TFT), non-local mind studies and other new sciences and integrates them into the practice of his Synergetic Therapy in New York City and Connecticut. He lectures widely across the United States and abroad, and has a weekly radio show on the Progressive Radio Network, Mindful Living with Dr. Henry Grayson.

His community service includes being the Co-Chairman of the PTSD Division of "Stand Up for Your Troops" Foundation to train providers to give effective services to returning military personnel. He has done self healing since the age of 25.

Please visit his web site is www.henrygrayson.com for more information.

BIBLIOGRAPHY

A Course in Miracles

Amen, Daniel, *Change Your Brain; Change Your Life*

Bender, Sheila and Sise, Mary; *The Energy of Belief*

Bach, Richard; *Illusions*

Barnett, Lincoln; *The Universe and Dr. Einstein*

Bohm, David; *Causality and Chance in Modern Physics*

Bohm, David; *Wholeness and the Implicate Order*

Boorstein, Seymour; *Clinical Studies in Transpersonal Psychotherapy*

Borg, Marcus; *Jesus and the Buddha*

Brody, Howard; *The Placebo Response*

The Buddha; *The Dhamapada*

Calder, Negil; *Einstein's Universe*

Callahan, Roger; *Tapping the Healer Within*

Capra, Frijof; *The Tao of Physics*

Carrington, Patricia; *The Power of Letting Go*

Chopra, Deepak; *Quantum Healing*

Church, Dawson; *The Genie In Your Genes*

Clark, Ronald, William; *Einstein: The Life and Times*

Cooper, Rabbi David; *God is A Verb*

Davies, Paul; *God and the New Physics*

Diamond, John; *Your Body Doesn't Lie*

Dhammapada; *The Sayings of the Buddha*

Diepold, John et. al.; *Evolving Thought Field Therapy: A Clinician's Handbook of Diagnosis, Treatment and Theory*

Dossey, Larry; *Recovering the Soul*

Dossey, Larry; *Space, Time and Medicine*

Dossey, Larry; *Healing Words*

Dossey, Larry; *Reinventing Medicine*

Einstein, Albert and Infeld, Leopold; *The Evolution of Physics*

Eliade, Mircea; *The Sacred and the Profane*

Emoto, Masaru; *Messages from Water*

Farell, Joseph Pierce; *Manifesting Michaelangelo*

Fienstein, David; *Energy Psychology Interactive* (cd learning series and manual)

Fienstein, David; Eden and Craig; *The Promise of Energy Psychology*

Frankl, Victor; *The Doctor and the Soul*

Frankl, Victor; *Man's Search for Meaning*

Frankl, Victor; *The Will to Meaning*

Gallo, Fred; *Energy Psychology*

Gallo, Fred and Vincenzi, Harry; *Energy Tapping*

Goswami, Amit; *The Quantum Activist*

Goswami, Amit; *The Self Aware Universe*

Goleman, Dan and Gurin; *Mindbody Medicine*

Grayson, Henry; *Mindful Loving: Ten Practices to Deepen Your Connections*

Grayson, Henry; *The New Physics of Love: The Power of Mind and Spirit in Relationships*

Green, Brian; *The Elegant Universe*

Hanh, Thich Nhat; *Collection Mind Body Medicine*

Hawkins, David; *Power versus Force*

Hawkins, David; *The Eye of the I*

Hay, Louise; *You Can Heal Your Life*

Heisenberg, Werner; *Physics and Beyond*

Heisenberg, Werner; *Physics and Philosophy*

Hora, Thomas; *Existential Metapsychiatry*

Hartung, John, Galvin, Michael and Gallo, Fred; *Energy Psychology and EMDR; Combining Forces to Optimize*

Holmes, Ernest; *The Science of Mind*

Jacobsone, Neil and Christensen, Andrew; *Acceptance and Change in Couple Therapy*

Jampolsky, Gerald and Walsch, Neale Donald; *Forgiveness: The Greatest Healer of All*

Jung, Carl and Paulie Wolfgang, ; *The Interpretation of Nature and the Psyche*

Justice, Blair; *Who Gets Sick*

Kaku, Michio; *Physics of the Impossible*

Kasl, Charlotte Sophia; *If the Buddha Dated: A Handbook for Finding Love on a Spiritual Path*

Krishnamurti, J.; *The Urgency of Change*

Krishnamurti, J.; *You Are the World*

Levy, Joel; *The Fine Art of Relaxation, Concentration, and Meditation*

Lipton, Bruce; *The Biology of Belief*

Look, Carol; *Attracting Abundance With EFT*

Luskin, Fred; *Forgive for Good*

Maharishi Mahesh Yogi; *Life Supported by Natural Law*

McTaggart, Lynn; *The Field*

Mijares and Khalsa; *The Psychospiritual Clinicians Handbook*

Mishlove, Jeffrey; *The PK Man*

Mollon, Phil; *EMDR and the Energy Therapies: Psychoanalytic Perspectives*

Nesse, Randolf, and Williams, George; *Why We Get Sick*

Newberg, Andrew; *How God Changes Your Brain*

Oschman, James; *Energy Medicine: The Scientific Basis*

Parnell, Laurel; *Tapping In*

Pearce, Joseph Chilton; *The Crack in the Cosmic Egg*

Pert, Candace; *The Molecules of Emotion*

Radin, Dean; *The Conscious Universe*

Roberts, Bernadette; *The Experience of No-Self*

Roberts, Jane; *The Nature of Personal Reality*

Roth, Robert; *Transcendental Meditation*

Russell, Peter; *The Global Brain*

Salzberg, Sharon; *Loving Kindness*

Sandweiss, Samuel; *Sai Baba: The Holy Man and the Psychiatrist*

Sarno, John; *Healing Back Pain*

Sarno, John; *The Divided Mind*

Segal, Inna; *The Secret Language of the Body*

Schnurr, Paula and Green; *Trauma and Health*

Schwartz, Gary: *The Energy Healing Experiments*

Shah, Idries; *The Way of the Sufi*

Shapiro, Francine; *Eye Movement Desensitization and Reprocessing: Basic Principles, Protocols and Procedures*

Sheldrake, Rupert; *A New Science of Life*

Shrodinger, Erwin; *What is Life?*

Siegal, Daniel; *The Mindful Brain*

Siegal, Daniel; *Mindsight*

Suzuki, Shunryu; *Zen Mind, Beginner's Mind*

Templeton, John; *Agape Love: A Tradition Found in Eight World Religions*

Thompkins, Peter and Bird, Christopher; *The Secret Life of Plants*

Thompkins, Peter and Bird, Christopher; *Secrets of the Soil*

Tiller, William, et.al.; *Conscious Acts of Creation*

Tillich, Paul; *The Shaking of the Foundations*

Tillich, Paul; *Systematic Theology*

Tipping, Collin; *Radical Forgiveness*

Tolle, Ekhart; *The Power of Now*

Tolle, Ekhart; *A New Earth*

Trungpa, Chogyam; *Cutting Through Spiritual Materialism*

Tzu, Lao; *The Way of Life*

Watts, Alan; *The Wisdom of Insecurity*

Watts, Alan; *The Book*

Willis, Harmon; *Global Mind Change*

Wheeler, John Archibald, Misner, Charles and Thorne, Kip; *Gravitation (Physics Series)*

Williamson, Marianne; *A Return to Love*

Wolf, Fred Alan; *Taking the Quantum Leap*

Yogananda, Paramahansa; *Autobiography of a Yogi*

Zukav, Gary; *The Dancing Wu Li Masters*

14941813R20202

Made in the USA
Middletown, DE
17 October 2014